W9-APS-282

ANIMATING DIFFERENCE

PERSPECTIVES ON A MULTIRACIAL AMERICA
Series Editor: Joe R. Feagin, Texas A&M University

The racial composition of the United States is rapidly changing. Books in this series will explore various aspects of the coming multiracial society, one in which European Americans are no longer the majority and where issues of white-on-black racism have been joined by many other challenges to white dominance.

Titles in the Series

ANIMATING DIFFERENCE

RACE, GENDER, AND SEXUALITY IN CONTEMPORARY FILMS FOR CHILDREN

C. Richard King
Carmen R. Lugo-Lugo
Mary K. Bloodsworth-Lugo

Rowman & Littlefield Publishers, Inc.
Lanham • Boulder • New York • Toronto • Plymouth, UK

Published by Rowman & Littlefield Publishers, Inc.
A wholly owned subsidiary of The Rowman & Littlefield Publishing Group, Inc.
4501 Forbes Boulevard, Suite 200, Lanham, Maryland 20706
http://www.rowmanlittlefield.com

Estover Road, Plymouth PL6 7PY, United Kingdom

British Library Cataloguing in Publication Information Available

Library of Congress Cataloging-in-Publication Data
King, C. Richard, 1968–
    Animating difference : race, gender, and sexuality in contemporary films for children / C. Richard King, Carmen R. Lugo-Lugo, Mary K. Bloodsworth-Lugo.
        p.   cm. − (Perspectives on a multiracial America)
    Includes bibliographical references and index.
    ISBN 978-0-7425-6081-9 (hardcover : alk. paper) − ISBN 978-1-4422-0195-8 (electronic)
    1. Stereotypes (Social psychology) 2. Motion pictures–Social aspects. I. Lugo-Lugo, Carmen R. II. Bloodsworth-Lugo, Mary K. III. Title.
    HM1091.K56 2010
    302.23'43083–dc22

                                                                        2009029813

For my grandfather, Oscar Larmer, for introducing me
to art, and to Abbey and Ellory for reminding me of the
power of imagination
CRK

To my students, who slowly begin to understand that
a talking fish is more than a talking fish, and a princess
is more than a princess
CRLL

For my granddad, Beauchamp Bloodsworth, in loving memory
of our many extended playtimes
MKBL

CONTENTS

ACKNOWLEDGMENTS

This book has many starting points. In part, it emerges from our professional interest in the interplay of racialization and sexualization in U.S. popular culture, no less than personal circumstances—King for instance watched most of these videos repeated times with his daughters, often worried about how they interpreted the racial projections as well as their white femininity. More specifically, it began to congeal in passing conversations about race and kinderculture. Subsequent discussions led King and Lugo-Lugo to organize special sessions on the subject at annual meetings of the National Association for Ethnic Studies and the Pacific Northwest American Studies Association. Our most immediate and initial note of gratitude goes to the participants—Lisa Guerrero, David Leonard, and John Streamas—for their insights and inspiration. Energized, we expanded our approach, making it more intersectional; focused our attention, emphasizing animated films; and drafted a proposal. Special recognition is due to series editor Joe Feagin, to whom we would like to extend our deep gratitude for his initial interest in this project, which proved fundamental to our success.

Less obvious, but no less important, have been the all too often invisible efforts of the faculty, students, and staff of the Department of Comparative Ethnic Studies at Washington State University. Whether posing questions that led us to rethink things in class discussion or managing finances, this book would look much different, and undoubtedly be inferior, without them. We benefited, moreover, from the efforts of the editorial and production staff at Rowman & Littlefield. In particular, Alan McClare, executive editor for sociology and anthropology, and Sarah Stanton, associate editor for sociology, deserve praise for their patience, prodding, and commitment throughout.

To our companions (human and otherwise), we owe special debts of gratitude that these words can only begin to repay. Their love and support have meant more than they know to us.

C. Richard King thanks his daughters, Ellory and Abigail, for sharing these movies and many other joys of youth, while continuing to ask hard questions. To his soul mate and better half, Marcie Gilliland, who is a rare jewel, he can only begin to express his gratitude for perspective—a presence which always challenged and comforted him.

Carmen R. Lugo-Lugo thanks her partner, Mary, for her support and encouragement and for always listening to her ideas about the world (animated or otherwise).

Mary K. Bloodsworth-Lugo thanks her partner, Carmen, and their mini-schnauzer, Emmy, for providing much love, family, and companionship.

Finally, we are grateful to Sage Publishing for permission to reprint "'Look Out New World, Here We Come'?: Race, Racialization, and Sexuality in Four Children's Animated Films by Disney, Pixar, and DreamWorks" in *Critical Methodologies/Cultural Studies* 9, no. 2 (April 2009): 166–78.

1

INTRODUCTION

In May 2009 Pixar released *Up*, its tenth animated feature. In many ways, the film confirmed the maturation of a genre that a decade before might have appeared to be little more than a marketing fad or technological gimmick. Reflecting previous productions from the pioneering studio, it combined engaging storytelling and sophisticated computer animation in a beautiful and evocative work that received much critical acclaim. The second of more than a half-dozen major animated releases in 2009, including *Dawn of the Dinosaurs*, the third installment of the *Ice Age* franchise, and *The Princess and the Frog*, much anticipated because of its black female lead, *Up* also attracted large audiences, premiered as the top-grossing film the week of its release, and netted more than $226 million in its first four weeks alone. Moreover, like many other titles in this genre, it sought to extend its profitability beyond the screen, primarily through marketing partnerships. In common with many animated features, especially those launched in the past decade, *Up* is not a fairy tale translated for new media and new sensibilities, but a complex narrative with human emotion and darker themes. As such, *Up* aims to appeal to adults as well as children. In short, Pixar's most recent release summarizes the state of animation today, underscoring the market forces, technological innovations, and cinematic themes central to its consolidation as a genre.

At first blush, it might appear that *Up* also confirms that the United States, as discernible in its popular cultural forms, has indeed entered an era after or beyond the difficulties of race, gender, and sexuality. After all, it features no princess in need of rescue or prince charming to slay the dragon; it contains none of the uncomfortable images of racial and ethnic difference so prominent (in retrospect) in some of the classics—such as the crows in *Dumbo*, King Louie in the *Jungle Book*, or the Siamese cats in *Lady and the Tramp*. However, such a reading of *Up* would be a misreading of the film and animated cinema over the past two decades—an argument we briefly rehearse here and elaborate throughout the remainder of the book.

Up focuses on the life of Carl Fredericksen (voiced by Ed Asner). Although set in the present, the past weighs on the narrative, particularly Carl's love for his childhood sweetheart and wife, Ellie, whose death leaves him alone and isolated in a quickly changing world and truncates their shared dreams of traveling to Paradise Falls in South America (modeled after Angel Falls in Venezuela) to shed the burdens of modern life. The turning of the movie is Carl's struggle to retain his autonomy, property, and memory of Ellie as the forces of development encroach upon him. Resisting a court order compelling him to be institutionalized, he engineers his escape by attaching thousands of balloons to his house, which literally lift him, and inadvertently a young scout named Russell, who has stowed away, up. After crash-landing near Paradise Falls, the odd couple set out to explore the environs, encountering a legendary tropical bird that Russell names Kevin. With the assistance of a talking dog they also encounter in the new land, the pair struggle to save Kevin from an unscrupulous explorer, idolized by Carl as a youth. In the end the adventure, driven by the force of heterosexual love, rejuvenates Carl, who changes from crotchety shut-in to community volunteer, becoming Russell's surrogate father in the process.

Up can be seen as a touching story and artistic triumph to be sure. But more importantly, the film underscores the ways in which animated films use difference without appealing to stereotypes to express prevailing understandings about human possibilities, social relationships, and cultural categories. Nearly a half century after the civil rights movement and the second wave of feminism, it centers on the adventures of two males (a boy and a man) transformed through the raceless, homosocial bond forged in the wild making the "right choices" as individuals, thus "doing the right thing," in this case, defending the defenseless. This is extremely important, given that Russell (the child) is Asian, yet his race is rendered invisible during the adventure. Russell's values, imparted to him by U.S. society, his family, and the Boy Scouts, are similar to those of Carl. Russell tells us he is basically fatherless, and seems to have a void his (Asian) mother cannot fill. The child is looking for a father and finds one in Carl's individualistic white masculinity. This story of white masculinity burdened with special obligations and tested in a hostile environment beset by evil reiterates the facts of whiteness and the race of masculinity. The setting of *Up* further underscores this racialized and gendered morality play: the threats of urban development and technology and the changes associated with them (integration, big government) provide an allegory and grounding for white male resentment, expressed daily on talk radio, cable news, and Internet chat rooms, while encouraging a kind of nostalgia for simpler times in which individual action mattered and entities like the Boy Scouts groomed young white men for their duties in life. Thus, Russell may not be white, but the institutions he belongs to (like the Boy Scouts) and his interactions with white men (like Carl and the unscrupulous explorer) are teaching him how to become an honorary straight white man. Moreover, Paradise Falls anchors not only Carl and Ellie's dreams, but a geography of difference in which exoticism, escape, and opportunity are projected onto a place in the South, surprisingly absent of indigenous people and surprisingly easy to get to and claim for yourself. Hence, the ideal space of imperial fantasy is open to the discovery of and in need of protection by (white) adventurers of the North. Finally, heterosexual romance and a failed quest for family propel *Up*, for it is desire for difference as much as attraction and commitment that bind Carl and Ellie to one another and compel Carl to repulse the force impinging on him as a white man by casting off the constraints of modernity and the chaos of change.

Our reading of *Up* points to many of the core issues we take up in *Animating Difference*. Specifically, in this book we seek to discuss the persistent interplay of race, gender, and sexuality in contemporary Disney, Pixar, DreamWorks, and Twentieth Century Fox films. Focusing on films released by each company since 1990, we also seek to analyze the impact these rehearsed themes have on the audience. *Animating Difference* goes beyond existing critiques of animated films by offering a thematic analysis, which gives us the opportunity to address a far greater number of films. Relatedly, we move beyond the heavy concentration on Disney by incorporating three other companies also engaged in the business of animated films. Our analysis is not exhaustive, as we do not analyze every movie released by these companies, but it is comprehensive, as we use multiple films to illustrate our points.

Our intersectional analysis of race, gender, and sexuality allows us to advance a nuanced discussion of these cultural texts and the social context in which they are created and consumed. At root, we argue not only that race, gender, and sexuality matter as themes or illuminate ideologies as many other critics have before us, but also that the interplay among them affords privileged insights into the cultural meaning and social structures that enliven them. Specifically, we assert that race and gender have shifted, taking on superficially positive qualities, which seemingly affirm and empower difference *and* retain significant force as a means of projecting fantasies, policing deviation, arranging hierarchies, grounding identities, and reinforcing exclusions. Moreover, we propose, it is the ways in which race and gender interface with (hetero)sexuality that encourages retrenchment and containment. Or, as Judith Halberstam (2008) has put it, romance and family constrain alternative vision and reinforce prevailing ideologies and identities.

Our readings of these texts in context turn on overlapping themes (naturalization, citizenship, collective memory, and the prospects of resistance) deciphered by identifying patterns in the narratives, characters, motifs, and messages of an array of animated films. Our approach emphasizes intersectionality given that race, gender, and sexuality do not have meaning or power alone but materialize and have significance in relation to one another; they are coproduced. Masculinity and femininity matter in relation to and through expressions of and enactments of citizenship, whiteness, blackness, Latinoness, and Indianness as well as heterosexuality. Moreover, our interpretative framework concerns itself with what is put into movies and what is left out by authors, as well as what is taken away or taken up by audiences. So we read these films for how they project ethnicity, sexuality, and gender onto characters, scenes, and stories, how, according to Halberstam (2008, 267), through imposition and juxtaposition they politicize characters, scenes, and stories. For instance, anthropomorphizing is crucial to many current animated films, endowing characters with personalities, and sexualized and racialized identities, which in turn shape the plot and animate the messages conveyed to audiences. Voices that project ethnicity or a dress that adorns gender are other examples to which we return throughout. Of course, animated films do not simply impose values or create meaning through allegories; they also actively encourage forgetting through distortion and erasure (the way Africa is pictured through animals and not people or American history is retold) or by unconsciously reinforcing the invisible norms of society (Why are there so few African Americans in animated films, not to mention excluded from lead roles?). This framework allows us to analyze images and ideologies, no less than practices and pedagogy.

DISNEY AND BEYOND

In this day and age, critics and consumers alike are less apt to see such cultural texts as innocently recast fairy tales. Instead, many commentators within and beyond the ivory tower now acknowledge, if only grudgingly, that animated films are more than mere entertainment or innocent amusements, and some would even rightly assert their reliance upon and recycling of racial, sexual, and gender stereotypes to tell stories and sell merchandise. In the academy, this realization has prompted a growing body of ever more sophisticated research into the cultural significance of Disney and the movies it produces. Indeed, this literature can be divided into two groups: (1) those works on Disney *in toto*, including animated films, as a *cultural complex*, and (2) those works that focus exclusively on the corporation's animated films through *cinematic critiques*. Among the former, we can list the following: Janet Wasko's (2001) *Understanding Disney*; Janet Wasko, Mark Phillips, and Eileen R. Meehan's (2001) *Dazzled by Disney? The*

Global Disney Audiences Project; Eric Smoodin's (1994) *Disney Discourse: Producing the Magic Kingdom*; and Sean Griffin's (2000) *Tinker Belles and Evil Queens: The Walt Disney Company from the Inside Out.* Among the latter are Elizabeth Bell, Lynda Haas, and Laura Sells's (1995) *From Mouse to Mermaid: The Politics of Film, Gender and Culture*; Brenda Ayers's (2003) *The Emperor's Old Groove: Decolonizing Disney's Magic Kingdom*, and Annalee R. Ward's (2002) *Mouse Morality: The Rhetoric of Disney Animated Film.* Regardless of the myriad tropes and analyses employed by these projects, and the sophisticated engagement with animated films and their products, the research that has been published on the animated world focuses almost entirely on Disney (the empire and/or the man).

We have long found these works inspiring for the manner in which they unravel the workings of ideology, the fabrication of identity, the formation of pleasure, and the play of power, which is why some of these works will help guide our discussion in the book. However, we have also come to believe that the singular focus on Disney, along with the discussion of isolated categories such as gender (to the exclusion of others, such as race), is limiting. As a consequence, in what follows, building on these earlier approaches, we formulate a more complex and complete understanding of the bundle of social relations, cultural meanings, and political projects anchoring and animating the production, circulation, and reception of animated films as texts and technologies.

In *Animating Difference*, then, we seek to provide a fuller account and richer interpretation of the significance of animated films that is at once inclusive (covering key features released by Disney, Pixar, DreamWorks, and Twentieth Century Fox during the past fifteen years), interdisciplinary (informed by the methods and theories from throughout the humanities and social sciences), intersectional (attentive to the coproduction and interpenetration of race, gender, and sexuality), and engaged (sensitive to the linkages among text and context, image and audience, critique and change). Throughout *Animating Difference*, we concern ourselves with the productivity of animated films, grappling with the ways in which they reflect and reiterate dominant presuppositions and preoccupations about race, gender, and sexuality, while illuminating the manner in which they actively intervene in and leave an indelible imprint upon social worlds. We conceive of animated features as meaning machines, or what Henry Giroux (1999, 84) calls "teaching machines," which "inspire at least as much cultural authority and legitimacy for teaching specific roles, values, and ideals [as] more traditional sites of learning such as public schools, religious institutions and the family." Consequently, this thematically organized monograph undertakes a novel project, shifting both the content and terms of debate about cinematic representation, ideological formations, and everyday cultural politics.

FOCUSING THE LENS

Animating Difference provides an in-depth analysis of ideas, ideologies, and meanings embedded in the storylines of contemporary animated films, unraveling the intimate connections among cinema and socialization, particularly at the intersections of race, gender, and sexuality. We have identified a total of five types of animated films released during the past fifteen years: (1) films for an adolescent or adult audience; (2) live action movies that include animated elements; (3) films adapted from television programs aimed at children; (4) films made exclusively for the home market and directed (primarily) at children; and (5) films made by Disney, Pixar, DreamWorks, and Twentieth Century Fox. On a general level, we are not concerned with the first four types of films. Examples and explanations for excluding the first four types follow.

Mainstream theater-released films for an adolescent or adult audience (for example, *Beavis and Butthead*, *South Park*, and *Team America*) are few in number, restrictive in audience (they all have "R" ratings), and not the sites of all of our foci (socialization/ pedagogy, signification/stereotyping, and struggle/contesting texts) precisely because of their restrictive nature; they are not family-oriented movies. Similarly, live action movies that include animated elements (for example, *Space Jam*, starring basketball legend Michael Jordan, and *Looney Tunes*, featuring Brendan Fraser and Jenna Elfman) are too few in number as well, which prevents us from establishing decisive patterns. They are also a hybrid genre that complicates our project too much, for we would have to address issues involving racialization, race/gender dynamics, and sexuality from two different angles: one involving the animated characters, and the other involving the "flesh and blood" ones. Films adapted from television programs and aimed at children (for example, *Sponge Bob*, *Jimmy Neutron*, *Rugrats*, and *Wild Thornberries*) are more numerous, but do not cross over audiences/markets; that is to say, they are not necessarily available to mainstream audiences. In addition, looking at such adaptations would entail looking at television programming, which would add a more complicated layer of analysis (by adding another genre of popular culture), blurring our focus, and ultimately distracting from our core project. Finally, films made exclusively for the home market and directed (primarily) at children (*Veggie Tales*, for instance) are overly narrow, making it difficult to examine representation and reception, given audience, distribution, and media attention.

This leaves us with animated films by Disney, Pixar, DreamWorks, and Twentieth Century Fox. We chose these films because they target children as their primary audience (thus, most of the messages, ideas, and meanings embedded in them are aimed at children). These films also have all been released in theaters, which means they have been made available to broad audiences across the United States. Finally, the marketing techniques employed by the producers have made them pervasive entities in our society.

Thus, *Animating Difference* is inclusive, critically assessing many of the key animated films made over the past fifteen years; interdisciplinary, not constrained by one scholarly tradition; intersectional, drawing together race, class, gender, and sexuality; and engaged, offering readings that signs, stories, and structures. *Animating Difference* contributes to the corpus of critical analyses centered on animated films in the following ways: the analysis and topic are current; the project develops an intersectional analysis of race, sexuality, and gender; it analyzes multiple films by developing a thematic organization; it moves beyond Disney; it moves beyond a mere textual analysis by emphasizing context (such as social ideologies) and its relationships with texts (that is, with the films); it moves beyond representation by foregrounding reception and explaining how audiences respond to those representations; and finally, the project examines the effects of animated films on society in general, given that animated films are not solely for children anymore—even if the primary messages are aimed at them.

OVERVIEW

In the next chapters, we further outline the significance of animated race, gender, and sexuality in contemporary cinema. Specifically, we delineate changes in animated films and their connections to shifts within social structures, political ideologies, and cultural narratives, while suggesting that social frames have proven fundamental to the place of racialization and sexualization in animated films.

Against this background, using socialization as a theoretical foundation, in chapter 3, we work through the interplay of racialization and sexualization through socialization, establishing the key terms and central themes of *Animating Difference*. Specifically, we argue that along with the types of messages outlined above, animated films offer children intricate teachings about race and sexuality. Thus, as socializing agents, these films guide children (in the United States) through the complexities of highly racialized and sexualized scenarios, normalizing certain dynamics while rendering others invisible. In fact, we argue that these films teach children how to maneuver within the terrain of "race" and "sexuality." It is our contention that films, in their role as agents of socialization, provide children with the necessary tools to reinforce expectations about normalized racial and sexual dynamics. In order to illustrate our points, we focus on four specific films for that chapter: *The Road to El Dorado*, *Shark Tale*, *Toy Story*, and *Dinosaur*. While discussing race and sexuality as intersecting markers within the context of each movie is our primary aim in the book, in the interest of clarity, we actually discuss each social marker separately in this particular chapter.

In chapter 4, we offer a case study of the ways in which nature and native life have proven to be safe and productive spaces for the reworking of commonsense understandings of race, culture, and history in post-civil-rights America. The noble savage and the wilderness have emerged in animated films as a fundamental context to offer seemingly positive accounts of identity and difference. Particularly, we focus on the articulations of nature, race, and history, contrasting films located in Africa, *The Lion King*, *Tarzan*, and the *Madagascar* franchise, and those set in North America, *Pocahontas*, *Spirit*, and *Brother Bear*. Our analysis points to important differences in how these films use nature and native life, but suggests that they work to let viewers off the hook, allowing them to defer the legacies of empire, even as they enjoy the privileges conferred by colonization.

Following up on those seemingly positive representations, in chapter 5, we examine what some scholars have dubbed a Latino boom in the 1990s United States, detailing its impact in animated cinema. The "boom," which included an unprecedented number of Latino/a celebrities (singers, actors, athletes) at the center of U.S. mainstream popular culture, and a relentless consumption of different aspects of Latino "cultures," spilled into animated films at the beginning of the new millennium. DreamWorks and Disney released, in 2000, two animated films that seemed to emerge from the Latino craze in the broader society: *The Road to El Dorado* and *The Emperor's New Groove*. It is our argument that even though these films were set in places other than the United States (*El Dorado* was set in a pre-conquest mythical New World land, and *New Groove* was set in the pre-conquest South American Andes), both films teach lessons about Latinos in the United States, and about whiteness within the context of historical events. Thus, in chapter 5, we examine the juxtapositions of Latinidad and whiteness as they take place in both animated films.

In chapter 6, we seek to illuminate the less noticed but more powerful production of whiteness as it applies to gender. We begin the discussion in this chapter by arguing that since Disney's release of *Snow White and the Seven Dwarfs*, *Cinderella*, and *Sleeping Beauty*, femininity in animated films has been cast as white. However, we continue, although more recent animated films seem to portray more nuanced femininities (and gender roles generally) than the earlier films mentioned above, these portrayals are still highly racialized. A compounding element we find in contemporary animated films is the articulation of (a U.S. white) citizenship. This chapter explores the connections between constructions of (white) citizenship and articulations of femininity in four particular animated films: *Mulan, Lilo and Stitch, Shrek,* and *Chicken Run.* In chapter 7, we focus more fully on the place of sexuality and gender roles in animated films. In this case, several recent films for children offer opportunities, at least on the surface, for progressive lessons regarding nontraditional expressions of sexuality and gender (*Ice Age* and *Shark Tale* present two examples), and opportunities to consider alternative family structures (*Dinosaur* and *Finding Nemo* illustrate this particular point). In *Shark Tale,* for instance, the character of Lenny is uncomfortable with the viciousness expected of sharks and seems to convey that it is "okay to be oneself," even if this means resisting a preconceived "nature." In *Dinosaur,* Aladar is adopted by a clan of lemurs, which implies that a baby dinosaur (or anyone) can find "family" with those unlike oneself. However, despite the potential for meaningful lessons vis-à-vis issues of sexuality, gender roles, and family structures, these characters are only able to sustain themselves within a narrative frame that is highly racialized and heterosexist. We argue that these films promote the view that progressive lessons in one arena (sexuality, gender, and family) are only afforded via a negotiation—that comparable lessons not be offered in another arena (race and ethnicity). Moreover, in all instances, moments of "difference" themselves are, in the end, reinscribed within a more traditional narrative.

Audiences increasingly offer vocal and critical assessments of animated features. Although many of these commentaries remain individual chatter on websites, more organized movements have arisen in response to specific features, agitating against visible racist stereotypes. In chapter 8, we bring together representation and reception to outline the contours of commodity racism and resistance to it in and around animated films. We are especially interested in directing attention to politicized consumption, namely vernacular or grassroots movements of consumers/citizens against the messages of animated films. Following a history of political consumerism in this context, we examine the boycott of Disney launched by evangelical Christians in the 1990s, protests of *Shark Tale* by Italian Americans, and critical analyses of *The Road to El Dorado*.

In the closing chapter, drawing on the soon-to-be-released *The Princess and the Frog*, we reiterate the significance of (dis)articulations of racialization, sexualization, and socialization in contemporary animated films. In particular, we highlight the defining features of white racial (hetero)sexist frames as illustrated in the resurgence of animated films.

2

"A WHOLE NEW WORLD"

Animated Films in an Unsettled and Interconnected World

In 1953, Walt Disney released *Peter Pan*. For more than a half century, the beautifully drawn animated feature has delighted audiences with its touching reflections on the innocence and allure of childhood, its fantastic, if formulaic, tale of the struggle between good and evil, and its memorable and marketable characters— Captain Hook, Tinker Bell, the Lost Boys, Wendy, and of course Peter Pan. While make-believe has made the adventures set in Neverland magical for audiences of all ages, it is the world outside of the story and its projection onto the silver screen that has made it meaningful. In fact, *Peter Pan* affords a keen glimpse into the workings of race, gender, and sexuality in animated films. For instance, in the scene immediately after Peter Pan has rescued the beautiful maiden Tiger Lily and subsequently expelled Tinker Bell, he gathers with the Darling children and the Lost Boys around a fire in the Indian Camp. Against a backdrop marked by teepees and totem poles that combines elements from distinct cultural traditions to convey a sense of generic Indianness, they all join in song and dance, seeking an answer to the perplexing question, "What Made the Red Man Red?" The assembled braves and chiefs, painted a bright red, discover the origins of phrases white audiences would have associated with American Indians, "how" and "ugh." They interweave invented gibberish that must have sounded Indian—such as the refrain "Hana Mana Ganda." Viewers learn the former indicate simple Native American speech, while the latter is the stoic utterance of a young groom upon first seeing his mother-in-law. Meanwhile, as a pipe circulates and the young men dance, Wendy is admonished by an older woman, "Squaw no dance. . . . Squaw gettum firewood," and a young man flirting with a young woman discovers he is tickling the chin of an obese and ugly older woman with only two teeth. The song climaxes as Tiger Lily dances before Peter Pan on a drum. Much to Wendy's chagrin, the Indian maiden kisses her new hero, turning him a bright red color, precisely as the chorus proclaims that just such a kiss caused an historic native prince to blush and Indians have been red ever since.

Forty-two years later, Disney released *Pocahontas* (1995), a seemingly different animated feature involving Native Americans. Whereas the comforts of whiteness paced *Peter Pan*, the uneasiness of difference structures *Pocahontas*, pivoting around the interactions between a native nation, the Powhatan, and English colonists. Rather than pure fantasy, *Pocahontas* purports to be rooted in history, offering a narrative of national origin. Much like *Peter Pan*, the film centers on romantic intimacies, specifically the relationship between Pocahontas and John Smith. Indeed, it suggests throughout that heterosexual love can overcome the obstacles to racial differences, peace, and understanding. Moreover, while *Pocahontas* rejects ugly images of indigenous women still acceptable in the 1950s, it too favors the princess modeled in accordance with white standards of beauty. Finally, the comical savages of *Peter Pan* have no place in *Pocahontas*, which prefers to foreground a shared humanness while emphasizing the bond between indigenous people and nature, especially through the relationship between the native heroine and two amusing animal companions, and more importantly the sage Grandmother Willow.

Although it may be tempting to cast the clear differences between these two movies in progressive terms—equality, empowerment, and/or inclusion apparently reflective of a lessening of negative attitudes toward women and people of color—*Peter Pan* and *Pocahontas* actually have much more in common, little of which would be deemed positive, directing attention toward the central themes of *Animating Difference*. For instance, the theme of heterosexual "relationships" informing both *Peter Pan* and *Pocahontas* demonstrates that even while narratives may superficially change, their lessons nonetheless find grounding through the significance and endurance of male-female encounters. Heterosexual relationships rehearse motifs of rescue, among other recurring themes, and while Peter Pan (a white male) rescues Lily (a Native American princess) in one way, John Smith (a white male) "rescues" Pocahontas (a Native American princess) in another. Likewise, while *Pocahontas* rejects one characteristic portrayal of indigenous women (old and ugly), it nonetheless adopts another (that of princess, more specifically, a princess in need of rescuing). The relationship between such (racialized) images of female characters and the male figures that engage with them in animated films demonstrates more than a simple playing out of stereotypical representations. Rather, the ways that race, gender, and sexuality intersect in these films serves to complicate analyses beyond everyday stereotypes. With the Indian maiden's kiss, in *Peter Pan*, Peter turns a bright red color. This blush (which reveals embarrassment and/or sexual anticipation) then offers a reply to the question of "the red man's redness"—an answer that acts to sexualize indigeneity itself. Further, these two films demonstrate a stubborn continuity in the process of socialization, where race, gender, and sexuality operate as important signifiers in the production of animated films.

ANIMATED FILMS IN CONTEXT

As a consequence, in the fifty years since Disney released *Peter Pan*, animated films have undergone profound transformations that make them extremely important cultural texts. Whereas animated films once were almost exclusively associated with Disney, aimed at and evocative of childhood, considered entertaining hand-drawn stories, and relegated to the bygone era in Hollywood, over the past twenty years, they have become an increasingly significant commercial and cultural force. In fact, in the 1990s, amid the culture wars and the digital boom, several major studios, Disney, Pixar, DreamWorks, and Twentieth Century Fox most prominently, began producing animated features with renewed zeal and with the assistance of novel computer technologies that hailed not only children, but also adults, turning them into true "family movies." In the process, these films emerged as a marketing nexus for the concentration of pleasures and the dispersal of products directed at children and collectors, offering financial stability for a rapidly changing entertainment industry. The significance of the new wave of animated films is summarized in part by their success at the box office: in March 2009, 17 of the top 100 highest grossing films of all-time were animated features, all released within the last twenty years.

As we argue in subsequent chapters, beginning around 1990, we witnessed the proliferation of animated films (many of them successful at the box office). Different from the earlier Disney movies that emphasized a moral or a message in common with the older fairy tales on which they were often based, these newer films focused on the characters, their trials and tribulations, and the path to overcoming those vicissitudes. Thus, these characters, we argue, move away from the simpler, two-dimensional drawings of earlier films and provide viewers with more sophisticated characters that, in many ways, deal with complicated events. In these constructions, contemporary animated characters undergo the hardships of human existence (even those who are not human), while simultaneously providing viewers with familiar lessons about sexuality, race, and gender, embedded within teachings about ideologies of American individualism (e.g., we should conquer our fears, we should accept ourselves as we are, or we should build character by overcoming obstacles). It is clear that these stories are powerful agents of socialization, as they ultimately teach very specific messages about what is good (and acceptable) and what is evil (and unacceptable).

Now, as in the past, animated films render dream worlds, providing dynamic contexts in which to work through fundamental contradictions, elaborate core ideological principles, and reinforce accepted understandings of cultural categories and the appropriate social relations between them, playing a fundamental role in the maintenance of the status quo (see, for instance, Artz 2004; Giroux 1999; Ostman 2004). And, as our foregoing discussion underscores, race, gender, and sexuality continue to give life to these meditations and mediations. Importantly, however, they do not do so in the same way, nor in the same milieu. Clearly both the technologies for animating difference and the circuits of production and consumption have changed, heightening the quality and sophistication of more recent films, intensifying the presence of characters and codes in the everyday lives of children and adults alike, and accelerating the creation and consumption of difference. Arguably, of greater significance, animated films today screen their fantastic fictions in a world marked by the aftermaths of struggle for racial, gender, and sexual empowerment, inclusion, and equality, and backlashes against them.

Put simply, the texts of animated films have changed, as have the contexts in which they are produced and consumed, and yet they continue to formulate narratives rooted in dominant discourses that perpetuate inequalities and exclusions (see for instance, Ayres 2003; Faherty 2001; Giroux 1999; Towbin et al. 2003). These changes are numerous but most clearly include (1) new languages for expressing difference, (2) heightened efforts to mediate debates about difference, (3) changes in production, particularly the rise of computer-generated animation and global outsourcing, (4) novel markets and marketing strategies, (5) a sociopolitical landscape struggling with the aftermath of struggles for identity, inclusion, and equality, (6) the culmination of systematic reworking of the economy to stress flexibility, mobility, speed, and global interconnection, and (7) generic mutations reflecting deeper shifts in popular sensibilities, including irony and intertextuality.

NEW LANGUAGES OF DIFFERENCE

In many respects "difference" has changed, or, better said, the manners in which individuals and institutions describe it, interpret it, and account for it have changed: appeals to biology have given way to culture and society; overt expressions of racism and (hetero)sexism have become taboo, replaced by covert and coded formulations; a stark division has emerged between behaviors, conversations, and performances for the public or on the front stage and those occurring in private or on the back stage; humor and intention increasingly "excuse" racist and (hetero)sexist thought and action; the rhetoric of emancipation and equality has been recoded to protect those in power (reverse racism); universalism and equivalence bleed out the differences that make a difference, converting identity, tradition, and/or community into a resource, a style, an experience equally available to all; and the connection between difference and context, history, and power is eviscerated, cutting loose the former from the latter as free-floating signs. In this context, animated films render their others through superficial features and essentialized qualities (distinctive fashion, pattern of speech, architecture, or relationship to nature), affirm universal humanity, erase power, and above all else accentuate the positive.

While the remainder of the text elaborates on this conjunction in depth, two brief illustrations here clarify the significance of this new language. Mindful of the imperial imprint in the Tarzan story cycle, replete with celebrations of white supremacy, Eurocentric renderings, and masculine desire clichés, Disney studios sought to recast the story, while preserving its core elements. To this end, it sanitized it; as a Disney spokesperson noted, "We would never dream of doing anything that would offend anyone. . . . It's going to be PC [politically correct], of course. It's a family picture," which meant it would "sidestep the racial issue by not including blacks at all" (quoted in Mayer 2002, 63–64). Literally whitewashed, the animated feature would avoid the racial dynamic at its core, thus avoiding controversy and allowing audiences to tell themselves they had surpassed the ugliness of race, even as the narrative reiterated its fundamental workings. Perhaps more boldly, *Pocahontas* actually takes up cultural differences, as mentioned previously and elaborated in chapter 5, but does so by essentializing and decontextualizing. As a consequence, even a retelling of an imperial encounter becomes a relatively happy and uplifting tale about a universal human experience and transcendental truth: love bridges cultures and dissolves differences.

NEW MEDIATIONS

The resurgence of animation over the past two decades depends on the creation of new media and increased demands for mediation, for cultural interpretations that can resolve the contradictions posed by fundamental challenges and subsequent rearticulations. Much like the interracial buddy film unfolded as an important means to grapple with changing race relations, while affirming the continued centrality and superiority of white men (Denzin 2002; Feagin, Vera, and Batur 2001), so too animated films have afforded occasions to re-present, reflect upon, and even reject unsettling projects. Indeed, it is not so much that animated films have articulated fully formed critiques of whiteness and masculinity or championed women and minorities, as such articulations would demand that producers take positions and engage in the debates gathered together in public discourse as feminism, multiculturalism, and the like. Rather, they opt to formulate flexible narratives open to the incorporation of sanitized differences and safe reinterpretations. Hence, in a series of animated films made over the past two decades women appear as more active and empowered agents, often defying authority, making their own choices, and stepping beyond conventional gender roles. Ultimately, as we detail in subsequent chapters, these portrayals continue to box women into dependent, sexualized, and supplemental positions, frequently reinscribed through heterosexual romance and racialization. Moreover, and again as we discuss subsequently, where some animated films have sought to elaborate critiques of consumerism or acknowledge the importance of imperialism to the American experience, they routinely blunt these reassessments by failing to question structures, practices, and experiences in relation or in context. In a very real sense, they appeal to a deep desire among a broad public to be beyond or over racism and sexism, while affirming the interpretive frames and structural arrangements that have not only energized them, but refused to interrogate and undo them as well.

MODES OF PRODUCTION/CIRCUITS OF CONSUMPTION

Animated films were once exclusively hand-drawn, requiring a large investment in human capital and a skilled workforce. The major investments of time and money demanded and limited their number and frequency. In 1995, Pixar wrought a sea change: it introduced computer-generated animation, a process which increased the pace, predictability, and profitability of animated features. In its wake, almost every film in the genre has been rendered digitally. More recently, studios producing animated films have played a leading role in globalization. Eager to cut costs, they have looked to outsourcing (Sreedhar 2009).

As the means of producing animated films have changed, so too have the ways audiences consume them. To begin, audiences have multiplied. Once almost exclusively drawn for domestic consumers, animated films are now produced for decidedly global audiences (Artz 2002). The recent success of *Kung Fu Panda* in China clarifies the growing importance of international markets, a point underscored in chapter 9. Moreover, where animation previously had associations with, if not relegation to, the world of children, today films are drawn for and consumed as eagerly by adults as children. This multigenerational audience, here and abroad, importantly, are as likely, perhaps more likely, to watch an animated feature at home—on cable, on demand, on DVD, and increasingly online. Away from the screen, almost every major studio release brings with it action figures, games, and increasingly video games. The films themselves have mutated: sequels have become commonplace; television programs have become increasingly lucrative (for instance, Disney incorporated a spin-off of *The Emperor's New Groove* into its Saturday morning lineup and Nickelodeon is developing a series featuring the penguins from the *Madagascar* films); and live action shows (*Disney on Ice* or *The Lion King* on Broadway come immediately to mind) have emerged as a new crossover possibility. Finally, as was the case with *Up*, even when toys or other ancillaries are more difficult to develop, film studios routinely establish marketing campaigns and corporate partnerships with multinationals better known for selling other products, perhaps only tangentially related to the film itself.

STRUCTURAL REARRANGEMENT

To our minds, it is neither surprising nor happenstance that animated films, all but absent for nearly twenty years, re-emerged as a powerful new cultural force around 1990. The boom in animated films that began with *The Little Mermaid* reflected a crystallizing, if still emergent, social context: a context emergent in the aftermath of anti-colonial and freedom struggles, the end of overt white supremacy and triumphant patriarchy, the exhaustion of political projects directed at justice and equality, the collapse of the metanarratives of modernity, the passing of industrial capital, the withering of the nation-state, the compression of time and space, the eruption of new media, the culture wars, the union of neoliberalism and neoconservativism, and most recently the quest for a new world order. This new social context has been variously described as late modern, postmodern, or liquid modern, post-civil-rights, and post-feminist, or more reductively as post-industrial, global, or fast capital. The terms (and the differences between them) matter less than the novel structures and relationships to which they refer. Twenty years ago, Hall (1991,

57–58) offered a visionary mapping of the then emergent structures, describing them as post-Fordism:

> Post-Fordism is a term suggesting a whole new epoch distinct from the era of mass production . . . [and] it covers at least some of the following characteristics: a shift to new information "technologies"; more decentralized forms of labor process and work organization, a decline of the old manufacturing base and the growth of the "sunrise," computer-based industries; the hiving off or contracting out functions and services; a greater emphasis on choice and product differentiation, on marketing, packaging, and design, on the "targeting" of consumers by lifestyle, taste, and culture rather than by categories of social class; a decline in the proportion of the skilled male, manual working class, the rise of the service and white-collar classes and the "feminization of the work force; an economy dominated by the multinationals, with their new international division of labor and their greater autonomy from nation-state control; and the "globalization" of the new financial markets, linked by the communications revolution.

These changing material conditions have contributed to the crystallization of novel signifying practices for the connecting, conveying, and circulating of difference and social power.

POSTMODERN FICTIONS

Although the resurgence of animated film initially dedicated itself to reworking the well-worn formula of Disney classics and translating canonical fairy tales for a new age, over time it incorporated broader cultural trends. These innovations reflected prevailing sensibilities, reinvigorating the genre and extending its reach. Until *Toy Story*, in 1995, animated features recycled two key elements of earlier films, like *Snow White* and *Cinderella*: they centered on a "princess" figure in a fantasyland, who even if empowered was saved by love, and they were musicals, often featuring songs that crossed over to the pop charts. With Pixar's initial release, however, all of this would change. While distressed damsels and the power of heterosexual romance persisted to a greater or lesser extent, animated features would draw on elements of what might be dubbed postmodernism to tell stories. Subsequent films became increasingly intertextual, ironic, irreverent, self-referential, and satiric. They not only abandoned the fairy tale, opting for contemporary (*Toy Story* and *Bolt*), future (*WALL-E*), and historic (*Spirit*) settings, individual films also parodied this storyline. For instance, much of the humor in *Shrek* turns on making fun of characters and tropes from well-known fairy tales. Moreover, at least since *Toy Story*, animated features have aggressively poached from popular culture and other animated films. *Shrek 2* incorporates the reality shows *Cops* and *American Idol*, and *Madagascar: Escape 2 Africa* draws explicit parallels with *The Lion King* to play with the genre and poke fun at its more reverential predecessor. The generic shifts, importantly, make the films more appealing to adults, ensuring broader audiences, because they make them more current, even hip.

FRAMING AND FRAMERS

The developments reviewed above have had a profound impact on animated films, even altering images of race, gender, and sexuality; however, as our juxtaposition of *Peter Pan* and *Pocahontas* at the start of the chapter underscores, these changes have not fundamentally altered stories or structures, which overwhelmingly center on and celebrate whiteness, masculinity, and heterosexuality and their purported superiority, while marginalizing, if not denigrating, those projected as different, whether abnormal or abject. To grasp this persistence and the role animated films today play in it, we must rethink dominant understandings of racism and (hetero)sexism. Far from being exceptional, antiquated, or individual, these arrangements and expression of power saturate American life, shaping the emergence and evolution of the United States. As such, they are routine and everyday phenomena, rooted in history, and shaped by social relations and cultural practices.

They are, according to Joe Feagin (2006), "systemic." Although Feagin concerns himself with systemic racism, he conceives its past and present formulations to be entangled with the patriarchal family, a position he shares with Abby Ferber and Patricia Hill Collins, who might prefer to refer to it as intersectionality. Whatever one names it, racism and (hetero)sexism take shape "in relation" to one another. Historically, anti-intermarriage laws and lynching in the South expose the powerful relationships between race, gender, and sexuality. They also point to the ways in which whites interpret, rationalize, and act upon their prejudices and preoccupations. That is a bundle of meanings attached to each individually and all collectively, so that black femininity or white masculinity had a particular significance, opened individuals, bodies, and spaces to specific sorts of actions, and explained or encouraged a narrow range of relations, greetings, and deportments. Race, sex, and gender congeal in particular sociohistorical conjunctures as a system—a way of seeing and a way of being in the world. Feagin (2006, 25–28; 2009) stresses the fundamental importance of what he calls "the white racial frame" to the contours and controls of this system, which as noted above is strikingly distinct from and painfully similar to the United States today.

This frame goes beyond mere ideology, according to Feagin (2009), because it weaves together cognitive, interpretive, emotional, and practical elements as well as sights, sensations, sounds, and even smells, imprinting individuals with a shared lens through which they organize and act upon the world around them through stereotypes, metaphors, images, emotions, and inclinations. It orbits around white actors and actions, applauds white ways of thinking and being, and embraces whiteness as the standard or norm and the superior or exception; at the same time, it conceives of non-whites as supplemental, alien, and transgressive, dismisses non-white achievements as substandard, deviant, and inconsequential, and implements projects intent to probe, problematize, and police non-white communities for their purported inferiority, deviance, and inhumanity. While reminiscent of Charles Mills's discussion of the "Racial Contract" and Theo Goldberg's account of racism as a state or structured condition associated with modernity, Feagin offers a pathway beyond intention and hate. Of special interest for us, the white racial frame, or framing to make it active, directs attention to the preoccupations, presuppositions, and practices through which certain images, ideas, and emotions enter the picture, become visible, take on meaning. We would prefer to reframe this frame, making it compound and plural—white heterosexist frames—to foreground its intersections with and interdependence upon sexuality and gender for its force and form and to recognize its multiple, polyvalent, and contradictory formulations. Whatever one prefers to call it, what is crucial to take away is that an organized set of dispositions, interpretations, codes, and emotions, anchored in a specific context, shape the projection of difference onto the screen. As such simply moving from a negative to a positive image of women, Latinos, children, vegetarianism, single fatherhood, or Native Americans, in and of itself, is insufficient, reflecting how the frame, in response to social pressures and moral panic, filters and focuses upon, emphasizes or erases, certain elements of the other. Thus, so long as gays and lesbians are demonized, excluded from marriage, beaten on the street, called names, and denied jobs or African Americans endure worse education and housing, more limited job opportunities, and increased incarcerations and murder rates, it is unthinkable they will be given fully human roles on-screen.

Moreover, so long as those conceiving of illustrating, plotting, editing, marketing, and enjoying such features are largely whites subscribing to and inscribing white heterosexist frames, the changes described in this chapter will be of little significance. To put this in more concrete terms: virtually every animated movie made over the past two decades has been made by EuroAmerican writers, directors, and producers for largely EuroAmerican audiences. As a consequence, in the making of *Pocahontas*, for instance, Disney ignored Powhatan advisors, who stressed the historical realities of EuroAmerican conquest and the inappropriateness of transforming the prepubescent Pocahontas into a nubile princess in an effort to craft an entertaining and profitable story. In the process, they created a film, according to Robert Eaglestaff, a Native American educator and principal in Seattle, that would unsettle creators and consumers alike if they saw it like many indigenous people did: it is "like trying to teach about the Holocaust and putting in a nice story about Anne Frank falling in love with a German officer" (quoted in Kilpatrick 1999, 151). This is an assessment that would no doubt horrify most who see the world through white heterosexist frames. At this moment, then, the capacity to critically discern these frames, as we outline in the next chapter, is all the more important.

HOW WE READ ANIMATED FILMS

In our subsequent interpretations of animated films, we employ an interpretive approach that combines a series of reading strategies that make connections and put bundles of meanings in relation to one category/event to discern the form and force of white racial (hetero)sexist frames. At root, because animated "movies manufacture the way we see, think of, feel, and act towards others" (Kellner 1995, 1), we have cultivated ways of "seeing" that read against the grain, refuse the accepted ways of looking, and prize techniques of reframing race, gender, and sexuality (see Denzin 2002). Thus, unlike many previous studies of this domain of popular culture, we do not emphasize stereotypes, favor one axis of difference, or concentrate on a single film. Instead, as we watched these movies, we looked for symbolic patterns, repetitions, intersections, silences, and gaps central to the creation of meaningful differences within and across movies.

This involves listening to the voices spoken for animated characters: Why does Puss in Boots have a Spanish accent? How does his accent inflect and reinforce images of exoticism, romantic heroism, and machismo? And would the film and its affects (amusement or desire, for instance) be the same if Puss in Boots did not have a Spanish accent? For us, it clearly pulls together in a naturalized way the ideas we have as a society about expressions of Latin masculinity as distinct, which in turn multiplies the uses of difference in relation to one another (e.g., Puss in Boots' masculinity in relation to Shrek's or to Donkey's).

Our reading of these films also entails sensitivity to the polyvalence of symbolic expressions. Whereas blackness empowers the creation of the cool, smooth, and decidedly marginal superhero Frozone in *The Incredibles*, it also enables the loud, obnoxious, and hypersexualized Stella the Skunk in *Over the Hedge*. Here, it is precisely the coupling of race with gender and sexuality that allows for these representations to take the shape they do. Indeed, it is precisely their relationship to white heterosexuality that sets them apart, as both features render staid family units as normal and central. Nevertheless, in these films, the nuclear family also is pictured as boring and mundane, something which youth rightfully rebel against and which adults commit themselves to in spite of its challenges (see Tanner et al. 2003). Moreover, even as the penultimate expressions of the white racial (hetero)sexist frames, these representations do not exhaust the power of racialization and sexualization. Heterosexuality also has a magical quality in many animated films: it brings happiness (i.e., they lived happily ever after), fosters desire (i.e., sexual anticipation can be seen in many male characters), and produces profound transformation (i.e., from human to ogre, from frog to human, from utterly miserable to blissfully content), and does so in ways that underscore the privileges of white masculinity (the gaze, desire, and dominance), the objectification of women (of color), and the impropriety of alternatives (Martin and Kazyak 2009).

In short, in the following chapters, we seek to reframe and deconstruct the many and varied ways animated features give life to difference. In so doing, like Hernan Vera and Andrew M. Gordon (2003, 8), we hope not only to offer a better understanding of individual films and the collectivity of animated films, but to have a keener sense of how race, gender, and sexuality matter in a society wildly entertained by animated features.

CONCLUSION

In this chapter, we have sought to provide a brief overview of the resurgence of animated films and why it matters. Stressing the interplay of text and context, we have cataloged the key ways that the production and consumption of difference within the genre has changed. We have also detailed the ways that framing as a structured, interpretive practice has circumscribed the capacity of animated films, directing them to reiterate white mythologies and heterosexist desire clichés. Against this background, in the next chapter, we encourage critical readings attuned to the contradictions of animated films and the sociocultural conjuncture that give them life and meaning. In particular, we detail the theoretical and methodological approaches that we bring to interpretations of race, gender, and sexuality, arguing against discrete readings of individual themes, singular texts, or ugly images and in favor of comparative, intersectional, and engaged accounts that link grounded patterns of signification across films to social structural arrangements.

3

"LOOK OUT NEW WORLD, HERE WE COME"?

Racial and Sexual Pedagogies

Released in 2005, the DreamWorks animated film *Madagascar* tells the story of a group of four spoiled and pampered animals from New York's Central Park Zoo (Alex the lion, Gloria the hippopotamus, Marty the zebra, and Melman the giraffe) who end up on the island of Madagascar after a complicated escape from the zoo and a shipwreck. Experiencing life in the wild leads the four friends to discover that they do not belong in the jungle, as they seem to prefer the comforts to which they had grown accustomed in the city.

Within a tale relating the adventures of cute and funny animals, the film weaves complicated stories about citizenship and subject positions juxtaposing the North (represented by New York City) and the South (represented by the Madagascar jungle). The fact that Alex, Gloria, Marty, and Melman feel uncomfortable in (and in fact are not able to recognize) the wild when they first arrive in Madagascar (Melman mistakes it for the San Diego Zoo) tells us that as residents of the post-industrial North part of the globe, these animals are foreign to the South, a place in which they should feel at home, but they actually find uncivilized. But home for them is New York and its comforts, and they become tourists in their new place, consuming the culture and influencing the lives of those subjects who do belong to the jungle of Madagascar (specifically, the lemurs who party constantly and the fossa who prey on the lemurs). This narrative of citizenship as (not) belonging, thus, becomes a "teaching tool" by which the audience learns about how they and others are positioned in relation to their nation-state, regardless of the fact that the main characters teaching them those lessons are actually animals.

Animated films, like any other cultural artifact, teach us "valuable" lessons, which is why we are, in this project, focusing on this particular genre, which is becoming a pervasive part of Hollywood. In fact, in the last decade or so we have witnessed a proliferation of successful animated films, the majority of which have been made by Disney, Disney and Pixar, and DreamWorks. Full of fantastic computer-generated images and special effects, the characters in these films depart from the simpler, two-dimensional designs in earlier (mostly Disney) films and provide viewers with more sophisticated, three-dimensional, emotion-displaying characters. Technological advances notwithstanding, these films, on a social level, offer viewers all-too-familiar and ordinary lessons wrapped in extraordinary and sometimes-magical plots. In a basic sense, the narratives embedded within these recent stories provide children (their primary target audience) and even adults with audio-visual reinforcement of ideologies concerning gender roles, the importance of conquering one's fears, the rewards of hard work, or the benefits of team effort, making these stories powerful agents of socialization. Elizabeth Freeman (2005, 85) actually describes these films as "'portable professors' of a sort, offering diagnoses of culture for adults even as they enculturate children." As mentioned above, these successful animated films also offer lessons about accepting ourselves for who we are, the wonders of pulling ourselves up by our bootstraps, and the idea that love conquers all—even seemingly insurmountable class differences, ill-intentioned acts, and evil characters. Similarly, the narratives teach very specific messages regarding clear-cut dichotomies such as good and evil; namely, that good and evil are mutually exclusive, self-contained monoliths, and that the good will always be good, while the evil will always be evil. Henry Giroux (1999, 2) explains this best when he claims that with these films, the corporations involved (for example, Disney, Pixar, and DreamWorks) are "regulating culture," and thus profoundly influencing "children's culture and their everyday lives." The messages embedded within these films resonate with children and are reiterated through other sources, while they also resound with parents who have received the same lessons since childhood. As Helaine Silverman (2002, 299) conveys, "As a quintessential form of American public culture, animated movies may be examined as a site where collective social understandings are created and in which the politics of signification are engaged." According to Giroux (1999, 2), these films are part of a popular culture that "is the primary way in which youth learn about themselves, their relationship to others, and the larger world." He goes on to argue that

> media culture has become a substantial, if not the primary educational force in regulating the meanings, values, and tastes that set the norms, that offer up and legitimate particular subject positions— what it means to claim an identity as male, female, white, black, citizen, noncitizen. (2–3)

Giroux insists that "entertainment is always an educational force" (28). Within this "edutainment," "animated films operate . . . as the new teaching machines" and "they possess at least as much cultural authority and legitimacy for teaching roles, values, and ideals as more traditional sites of learning" (84).

In this chapter, we argue that, as suggested by Giroux, animated films offer children intricate teachings about race and sexuality. Thus, as socializing agents or "teaching machines," these films guide U.S. children through the complexities of highly racialized and sexualized scenarios, normalizing certain dynamics and rendering others invisible in the process. We fundamentally disagree with Bell, Haas, and Sells (1995, 7), who argue that "Disney's trademarked innocence operates on a systematic sanitation of violence, sexuality, and political struggle concomitant with an erasure or repression of difference." To the contrary, these films precisely teach children how to maneuver within the general terrain of "race" and "sexuality," and they highlight quite specific differences. It is our contention that films, in their role as agents of socialization and "portable professors," provide children with the necessary tools to reinforce expectations about normalized racial and sexual dynamics. In order to illustrate our points, we will focus on four specific films: *The Road to El Dorado* (2000), *Shark Tale* (2004), *Dinosaur* (1993), and *Toy Story* (1995). We could discuss race and sexuality as intersecting markers within the context of each film, but in the interest of clarity, we will discuss each category separately here.

CON MEN AND FISH: RACIALIZED REPRESENTATIONS AND ANIMATED FILMS

In her book, *Understanding Disney*, Janet Wasko (2001) lists the various elements found in any "classic" Disney narrative: style, story, characters, and themes/values, along with the formulaic components of each. We would like to focus on her description of characters, for it is through the characters that "we" piece together the story, learn the themes/values, and get a feel for the film's style. According to Wasko, Disney anthropomorphizes animal characters, presents formulaic heroes, heroines, and villains, and provides stereotypical representations of gender and ethnicity. We can offer two points in relation to Wasko's basic claims. First, Wasko's description of Disney's animated characters can likewise be extended to the animated characters in films made by DreamWorks and Pixar (as we will discuss in this chapter); and second, her claim regarding stereotypical representations can be expanded in the following way: even though animals (and other non-human characters) are anthropomorphized in children's animated films, these films also, unfailingly, racialize non-human characters in the process. That is to say, these characters are not simply transformed into some generic "human" (for there are no generic humans); rather, they are inscribed, for example, as white "humans," black "humans," Asian "humans," or Latino "humans." Thus, we maintain that animal and other non-human characters undergo a kind of racialized anthropomorphism within animated films. Our discussion of *Shark Tale*, below, will illustrate this point.

Similarly, although human characters in animated films still "play" formulaic and stereotypical roles and adhere to strict dichotomies, the scope of these roles and the shape of these dichotomies seem to be broadening in recent films, adapting to contemporary definitions. We will use *The Road to El Dorado* to illustrate this point. Consequently, we also argue that while many "classic" animated films (often featuring human characters) tend to adhere to strict dichotomies (good/evil, hero/ villain, etc.), there are also recent notable examples (generally featuring anthropomorphized characters) that create more nuanced constructions of these binaries. That is to say, while we still see films that enact clear sets of binaries and simultaneously racialize characters in accord with these roles, we are also witnessing very recent films that complicate classic structures. The two films discussed in this section provide examples of each sort of film.

Stereotypes and Dichotomies in *The Road to El Dorado*

We begin our discussion with a film that conforms to classic structures and dichotomies: DreamWorks' *The Road to El Dorado*. Adding to Wasko's discussion of stereotypical representations of race and ethnicity in children's films, and—we add—sexuality, we argue that stereotypical representations must be placed within a broader, more complicated historical context within which gendered, racialized, and sexualized dynamics take place. In other words, stereotyped representations are only relevant because they simultaneously reinforce both contemporary and historical notions of race, gender, and sexuality. Let us take, for instance, representations of race in *The Road to El Dorado*.

Set during "the conquest" of the Americas, *The Road to El Dorado* begins in Spain and moves to a mysterious location in what is now known as Mexico. The film begins with Hernán Cortez delivering a speech just prior to his departure for "the New World," in which he boasts, "We sail to conquer another world, for Spain, for glory." Thus, in a superficial way, the film subtly points to the greed-induced injustices of the Spanish Conquest; however, when examined more closely, *The Road to El Dorado* tells a highly racialized and dichotomized story involving Spaniards and indigenous peoples in the Americas. This story is accomplished by romanticizing the Indigenous as childlike and innocent beings (always smiling, rarely speaking, and mostly in awe) who are positioned as being in need of rescue. This "rescue" comes in the form of Tulio and Miguel—the "good" kind of Europeans (and the contrast to Cortez, the "bad" kind).

In the case of *The Road to El Dorado*, the evil characters are hopelessly evil (that is, Cortez and the high priest) and the good characters are ultimately good (that is, Tulio/Miguel and the chief). While Tulio and Miguel (described by DreamWorks as "a pair of two-wit con men") may sometimes lack good judgment, they are—in the end—good, decent people (as they *must* be given their place within the binary structure). Hernán Cortez, in his evil incarnation, becomes the damnation of the natives, while Tulio and Miguel discover their role as saviors of the doomed indigenous society.

The most interesting feature of Tulio and Miguel's characters is that, mistaken for gods, they are able to become heroes and save the indigenous society from its own heartless high priest. In fact, in his role as one of the gods, and responding to the high priest's request for a human sacrifice, Miguel gives the natives their first commandment: "There will be no sacrifices, not now, not ever." In the film, El Dorado (the place) becomes a site of racial dynamics where the indigenous population not only dances, drinks, and is happily festive, but also partakes in "uncivilized" practices such as human sacrifice. It is also in El Dorado that Spaniards Tulio and Miguel (with their puzzling British accents) manage to save the place, even after Miguel informs the chief that the Indigenous will not be able to fight off Cortez and his men, who are rapidly approaching the city. Despite this claim, Tulio is able to arrive at a solution to save the city that entails blocking its only entrance, thus preventing Cortez (or anyone else) from ever finding the city. In turn, its residents are isolated from other human contact forever, thus repositioning them as perpetually innocent and childlike peoples in need of protection.

While carrying out the plan, both "con men" renounce the gold they had planned to take, signaling a change of heart concerning their own greed and revealing that in the end—and different from Cortez—they *do* possess kind hearts. Nonetheless, given that Tulio and Miguel were "con men" who arrived and stayed in El Dorado through deceptive actions, their portrayal as ultimately kind-hearted heroes broadens any former (and pure) construction of "the hero." Moreover, dichotomies notwithstanding in *The Road to El Dorado*, Europeans become both the damnation and the salvation of the indigenous characters.

Racialized Anthropomorphism in *Shark Tale*

We find an excellent example of racialized anthropomorphism in the recent DreamWorks' film *Shark Tale*, in which Oscar, described by DreamWorks (2005) as "a little hustler fish," speaks in a clearly "black" American accent and lives in the ghetto part (South side) of the reef. His blackness is found not only in his accent and place of residence, but also in his mannerisms, behavior, and jewelry (that is, "bling"), which are highly racialized signifiers. For instance, in one scene, Oscar tries to "hustle his way" out of a situation with his boss, Sykes, a puffer fish. Oscar tries to connect with Sykes by performing a complicated "fin shake," but Sykes is unable to follow the steps. After a few attempts, Oscar gives up and says, "Don't sweat it; a lot of white fish can't do it." For children who are learning the intricacies of race (as a social signifier) and race relations, labeling Sykes as a "white fish" (and therefore Oscar as a "black fish") validates other societal messages. Children learn that our culture is strictly raced and racialized, since even fish can be black *or* white.

In fact, Oscar and Sykes are not the only fish racialized in *Shark Tale*. We can also find Ernie and Bernie (two Rastafarian jellyfish, complete with Jamaican accents) who work for Sykes; Lino (an Italian-American-accented Mob shark and master of the reef), and Mrs. García (an overweight, middle-aged, single, Mexican-accented female fish, with permanent rollers in her hair) who also lives in the ghetto. These are just a few examples. However, we can also locate nuances in the ways that these characters are racialized. For instance, not only is Oscar racialized as black, we can also see an ethnicization of race whereby Oscar is constructed as a black *American*. This ethnicization is accomplished through his juxtaposition to Ernie and Bernie, with whom he interacts. In one scene, for example, Oscar attempts to sing reggae, to which Ernie retorts, "Don't like the way you sing that song, man." In this way, Oscar is reinscribed as black, but this reinscription is promoted through contrasting Oscar, as black American, with Ernie and Bernie, as black *Jamaican* (where to be Jamaican means to be accepted by Rastafarian jellyfish). In addition, Sykes is actually finally able to perform the fin shake, once Oscar becomes a celebrity and Sykes becomes his manager. With Oscar's celebrity and Sykes's newfound investment, we see Sykes now able to do the fin shake and to speak "black lingo." We could argue that Sykes's "black performance" parallels that of white rap producers and others who "learn the lingo" to have better rapport with their "investments." In *Shark Tale*, furthermore, we witness ethnicization in "white," for Lino is not only racialized as white, he is ethnicized as Italian by way of very specific signifiers. For instance, Lenny (his son) tells Oscar that Lino is the godfather, Lino speaks with an accent usually associated with New York Italians, and Frankie (Lino's other son) receives a Catholic burial, performed in Latin, after he dies. While almost silly, these stereotypes serve as important signifiers of a particular *kind* of whiteness within the United States—the whiteness of a group that, until recently, was *not* actually seen as white.

DINOSAURS AND TOYS: STRAIGHTNESS, HETEROSEXISM, AND ANIMATED FILMS

A few years ago, Tinky Winky (of the children's television show *Teletubbies*) was rendered a "homosexual" by Jerry Falwell. Falwell—a professed straight man—claimed to know the status of Tinky Winky vis-à-vis "his" sexuality. Even though Tinky Winky never said, "I am gay," Falwell thought that Tinky Winky's color (purple) and his accessories (his purse) said, "I am gay" very clearly; Tinky Winky need not utter the words. It is worth noting, in this case, that Falwell's assessment of Tinky Winky also followed a curious path: He first assigned Tinky Winky a sex (male), then assessed that sex (by reading the color and the accessory as "inappropriate" gender attributions for a male), and then conflated gender and sexuality (by labeling Tinky Winky a "homosexual" on the basis of these "inappropriate" gendered characteristics). In addition, it could be the case that Tinky Winky's triangle headpiece clinched the "homosexual" assessment for Falwell.

At the time of the Falwell incident, some members of the gay and lesbian community argued that cartoon characters *do not have* sexualities; hence, in musing over children's television programming, Falwell had "simply gone too far." This was a case, some gay men and lesbians argued, of homophobia run rampant. However, it seems undeniable that cartoon characters—especially in Disney, Pixar, and DreamWorks productions—certainly do have sexualities, which is to say, they have *hetero*sexualities. Despite a tenuous relevance, or an outright irrelevance, to the story lines, "heterosexuality" (in the form of heterosexual relationships, or heterosexually oriented banter) pervades most films for children. Indeed, if there is a purpose to these seemingly pointless scenes, the aim could be taken to be the "indoctrination" of children into "the heterosexual lifestyle."

In the films discussed above, *The Road to El Dorado* and *Shark Tale*, we can easily find examples of heterosexual relationships and banter. In *The Road to El Dorado*, Tulio, who has warned Miguel regarding the dangers that Chel (the "native") could bring, ends up falling for her himself. The fact that it is Tulio, and not Miguel, who cannot resist the indigenous woman only underscores her danger, for Tulio is represented as the more level-headed member of the con men pairing. Upon first seeing Chel, after all, it is Miguel who states, "Maybe we should call this place 'Chel Dorado,'" while uttering sounds of sexual excitement. The introduction of Chel into the narrative occurs after a series of scenes in which the sexuality of the two main characters could be construed as unclear; for example, after the two men have recited to each other that they have made each other's lives more adventurous and rich (upon thinking that death was imminent) and after the two men have bathed naked together (upon arriving in "the New World"). Chel clarifies for the audience that these two men are, indeed, sexually "normal." Of course, this "normalcy"— played out in the relationship between Chel and the two Spaniards—also tells the audience that the indigenous woman is available for the white man's choosing, and that like El Dorado itself, no "normal" man could resist her temptation (leading to her/its conquest and possession).

In *Shark Tale*, the role of "woman as temptation and trouble" is played by Lola, who is positioned as a danger to Oscar's potential wealth as he places a "sure bet" on Lucky Day to win the ensuing seahorse race. As Oscar turns around and sees Lola seductively entering the room, a song unleashes the lyrics, "Better watch out, she'll take your cash. She's a gold digger." Of course, in *The Road to El Dorado*, Chel's initial interest in Tulio and Miguel also centers on the "escape" that they might offer, and she makes a deal with them to gain a share of their gold. However, in *Shark Tale*, the "type of woman" represented by Lola is also contrasted with two other sorts of women—the kind of woman with whom a man should eventually settle down (Angie), and the kind of woman that no "normal" man could find alluring (Mrs. García). Angie, unlike Lola and unbeknownst to Oscar, loved Oscar before his newfound life of fame and fortune. Oscar initially overlooks her affection, referring to her simply as his "best friend." But it is precisely one's best friend (as long as that best friend is of the "opposite" sex) who offers a man long-term possibilities, unlike the seductress who will leave him on a whim. Or, perhaps worse still, it is the "Lola type of woman" who will seek revenge if he leaves her first. Lola herself states that the only thing she likes better than money is revenge.

However, it is not Oscar, the film's main character, who is in the opening scene of *Shark Tale*. Rather, it is Lenny—the son of Lino, the "don" of the reef. As a worm struggles on a fishing hook, eyeing Lenny swimming closer and closer (with the theme to *Jaws* playing), the audience senses the danger. But Lenny does the unexpected. Instead of gobbling down the worm, he releases it from the hook and lets it swim free. As we learn, the thought of eating any of this "meaty" sea life makes Lenny sick. Lenny eventually confides in Oscar, in a discussion that evokes a narrative of self-outing, that he is a vegetarian. However, his family has known for some time that something is "odd" with Lenny—he is not a "normal" shark. As Lino says to Lenny, "You. I'm hearing things. When you look weak, I look weak," and "Son, you're going to learn to be a shark whether you like it or not." Thus, being a "normal" shark is equated with being a shark as such, and being a shark means being a vicious master of the reef (and not a compassionate consumer of kelp). Lenny's brother, Frankie, likewise tells Lenny, "If you want to make dad happy, you've got to kill something. You've got to be a shark."

While the issue of Lenny's sexuality is left open in *Shark Tale*, parallels between stereotypical representations of gay men and characteristics displayed by Lenny are played upon throughout the film. Not only does Lenny "come out" to Oscar (as a vegetarian), he also dresses both as a cowboy and as a dolphin at one point in the film ("Sebastian, the Whale-Washing Dolphin"). This "dress up" evokes both the fondness for uniformed men within gay male culture (the most famous example being the array of figures represented by the Village People) as well as the more general relationship between gay men and drag. When Lino sees Lenny dressed in this getup, he asks of Lenny, "What are you wearing? What *is* that? Do you have any idea how this looks?" Of course, while Oscar makes a plea for Lino's acceptance of Lenny at the end of the film, asking, "Why can't you love him as he is?" it is precisely Oscar who has subtly rejected Lenny at an earlier point in the film, stating the number one rule for friendship as "none of that snuggly buggly stuff. Whatever that was." Oscar thereby distances himself from any "abnormal" closeness between the two male characters (or two men in general) and designates such closeness as "icky." In fact, such intimacy is to be so desperately avoided that this particular rule for friendship is cited before rule number two—the rule directly related to Oscar's self-preservation: "If you ever have a change of heart [about being a vegetarian], please don't gobble me down." With his rules for friendship, Oscar reconstitutes himself as the heterosexual man—the man who may have other men as friends (as do Tulio and Miguel), but whose sexual desires are firmly positioned where they *should* be.

A point of connection between the overall representations of sexuality in both *The Road to El Dorado* and *Shark Tale* involves the incorporation of [hetero]sexuality into the narratives of the films when the basic messages could have been served without it. In this respect, children's films do not function very differently from adult-centered Hollywood films, which find a way to work a [heterosexual] love story into almost any plot. But unlike adults, whose sexualities have already been soundly established (it would appear), children are still learning the societal lessons of [hetero]sexuality—that heterosexuality is the "normal" sexuality and the desired outcome for "any healthy child." Thus, the seemingly unnecessary incorporation of heterosexuality into the narratives of children's films can actually be seen to serve a function. That is, it reiterates lessons that children receive elsewhere—that boys like girls and girls like boys, and men like women and women like men, even when the boys/men and girls/women are, for example, fish . . . or dinosaurs or toys.

[Needless] Heterosexuality in *Dinosaur*

In the film *Dinosaur*, the main character, Aladar, becomes orphaned when a bird picks up his egg and drops it far from Aladar's home. Aladar (a dinosaur) is subsequently adopted and raised by a clan of lemurs. While this unusual situation could, and perhaps does, offer lessons about "alternative families" or "families of choice," this message is fundamentally undermined given its repositioning within a framework of normative heterosexuality. This framework renders procreation the only legitimate reason for sexual activity and the nuclear family as sexuality's only "natural" outcome. For instance, near the beginning of the film, a scene with questionable relevance to the plot unfolds (the plot being dinosaurs making their way to the "nesting grounds" after meteors strike and destroy much of the Earth), when pairs of male-female lemurs are shown "doing the wild thing." While an argument could be made for the relevance of this scene (that is, it suggests the means of survival for a species, thereby foreshadowing the meteor scene, which renders extinction possible), any such significance—in our view—is undermined by a blatant depiction of lemurs "doing it."

To prepare for the mating ritual, we see Zini (Aladar's "brother") practicing his pickup lines, remarking, "Girl, I'm the professor of love. And school's in session," and "Hey, sweetie. If you'll be my bride, I'll groom ya." At the same time, we hear the girl and boy lemurs being taught their separate mating lessons. The girls are told to be subtle with their intentions and to "keep the boys guessing." Of the boy who has successfully mated in the past, we hear the praise, "He put the 'prime' in primate." And, as the boys arrive to "go at it" with the girls, we are privy to their introduction, "Here's your buffet table of love." All of the lemurs then embark upon heterosexual pairings, and all are successful, except for Zini, who reassures himself by saying, "Before you know it, she'll be wanting a bigger tree" (that is to say, "women are trouble"). Zini is appointed the only bachelor of the clan—except for Aladar, who has not yet found others "like himself" (that is, other dinosaurs). Thus, Zini and Aladar can be seen to form a connection on the basis of their mutual bachelorhood, and while Zini is unsuccessful with the ladies himself, he does not fail to offer advice to Aladar later when he meets Neera on the way to the nesting grounds. Zini remarks, "Hey, hey, there's your girlfriend. What you need is a little help from the love monkey." Finally, Aladar is able to settle down with "the right girl," and the two dinosaurs have "a little Aladar" who "looks just like his father." In the film's final scene, we see Zini encircled by a "harem" of female lemurs, suggesting that he too might finally mate successfully. Zini asks, in a moment of sexual excitement, "Are you ladies up for a game of monkey in the middle tonight?" His inquiry is followed by a cheesy grin of sexual anticipation.

The Love of Toys in *Toy Story*

Another example of heterosexual incorporation into a children's film can be seen in the popular *Toy Story* movies, in which the voice of Tom Hanks animates the character of Woody. In the opening scene of *Toy Story*, Woody's "boy" (Andy) acts out a playtime scene in which Woody saves the life of Little Bo Peep's flock. When Andy leaves his bedroom, all the toys come to life. Little Bo Peep gently whispers to Woody, kisses him, and thanks him for saving her sheep. She follows this gesture with the line, "What if I get someone to watch the sheep tonight? Can you come over?" Woody blushes, revealing his sexual anticipation through the cheesiness of his smile (much like Zini). At the end of the film, Little Bo Peep tells Woody, "Merry Christmas, Sheriff," as she pulls him toward her with her shepherd's hook. To her holiday greeting, Woody replies, "Hey, isn't that mistletoe up there?" The two toys then disappear, out of the frame, as the film closes.

This final scene arrives after Woody, throughout the film, has found himself having to compete not only for the affections of Andy but also for those of Little Bo Peep. While Woody was previously the mainstay of both Andy and Little Bo Peep, their loyalties are tested as Andy's new toy, Buzz Lightyear—the new and flashy sort of toy (guy)—enters the scene. Given that Andy's family will be moving to a new home in just a week, Woody has instructed the toys to locate partners for the move. Woody wants no toy to be lost or left behind. With the arrival of Buzz Lightyear, on the occasion of Andy's birthday, Little Bo Peep thinks that she has found her solution. As she remarks upon first noticing Buzz, "I've found my moving buddy." Little Bo Peep thereby displaces Woody from the role that he would have likely assumed. In the end, however, Little Bo Peep returns to Woody, much as Oscar returns to Angie (in *Shark Tale*). The message, here, is that the steady guy—rather than the flashy one—is a girl's best option. While flashiness might offer temporary excitement, steadiness provides long-term stability. The "tried-and-true" is ultimately better than the "toy-of-the-day." It is worth noting that in a sustained *Toy Story* subplot, Mr. Potato Head spends the entire film awaiting the arrival of Mrs. Potato Head. She finally appears at the end of the film, on the occasion of Andy's sister's birthday.

The arrival of Mrs. Potato Head is then followed by the regular appearance of the united and happy couple throughout the film's sequel, *Toy Story II.*

CONCLUSION

Given such depictions of race and sexuality enmeshed within the story lines of films primarily intended for children, it seems reasonable to maintain that racialization—including racialized anthropomorphism—takes place on various levels within these animated films. On a basic level, such films provide children with important signifiers that chart racialized, and *racist*, dynamics. On a more profound level, these films serve as tools that help to teach children to maintain the racial (and racist) ideologies that maintain the status quo. For instance, even though Oscar is no generic fish, we are taught that he should nonetheless be happy to be a fish (a black fish), to live in the ghetto, and to enjoy the lot assigned to him in life. As Oscar, at the end of *Shark Tale*, settles into his newfound life as co-owner of the Whale Wash (with Sykes), we note that while he has indeed moved from his father's lot as longtime tongue scrubber, he has not risen so far as to make a white audience uncomfortable with the success of a black man/fish. After all, Oscar shares his bourgeois success with a white man, Sykes. Similarly, in *The Road to El Dorado*, we learn that the conquest of the Americas is over, and there is the possibility that multitudes of indigenous folks did not die after all. Rather, their civilizations may actually be hidden behind large rock formations and impossible for us to find—thus we need not feel guilty about the extermination of entire cultures. We need not worry about rape either, for we are told that indigenous women were actually more than willing to leave their families to live adventurous lives with European men (as demonstrated by the relationship between Chel and Tulio). And slavery, we are instructed, was an institution for evil people who fundamentally deserved it (as depicted by the enslavement of the high priest by Cortez).

Moreover, there is an ethnicization of race in more recent animated films for children, suggesting that children are not only being taught "crude" racial categories but more intricate ways of conceiving "race" in relation to ethnic markers. While it might be argued that there are positive aspects to such portrayals (for instance, they complicate race by not homogenizing racial categories such as "black" or "white"), we would argue that the real purpose of the ethnicization of race—in a film like *Shark Tale*—is to differentiate characters in not-so-positive ways. For example, Lino (Italian white) is contrasted with Sykes (nondescript white) in ways that promote negative stereotypes of Italians in comparison to "other" whites. While Sykes may wish to exploit Oscar and his newfound fame, Sykes is himself victimized by Lino's perpetual bullying, thereby rendering Sykes a "better" kind of white fish than Lino.

Heterosexism plays a similar role within these films, for a heterosexist lens implies *no* sexuality where a case can be made for glaring *hetero*sexuality. Owing to the fact that heterosexuality is normative, depictions of it often go unnoticed. This claim seems a more accurate reflection of the actual status of sexuality within children's animated films than the position that animated characters have no sexualities. All of the main characters discussed above not only have (hetero)sexualities but also convey more nuanced lessons from within the category "heterosexual." That is to say, Oscar's attention is depicted as properly directed at *women*, while ultimately, he must end up with the right *kind* of woman; Woody must compete for the affections of Little Bo Peep, while she is distracted by the flashiness of the wrong *sort* of man. Even when a character is introduced, like Lenny, whose sexuality is unclear, this lack of certainty only affords the sort of mild put-down illustrated by Oscar's "none of that snuggly buggly" comment. With this distancing remark, heterosexuality is recentered and given its rightful place as the only "normal" sexuality. In the case of Tulio and Miguel, any lack of clarity regarding the nature of the male-male relationship is resolved through the introduction of Chel, the irresistible woman.

Likewise, rather than construing animated characters as generally unmarked by race, it is more likely that these characters are raced as white (which is why mainstream audiences do not notice many characters' races) as well as non-white (which is why other characters jump from their backgrounds). Concerning the second part of this point, we might consider Native Hawaiian Lilo in Disney's *Lilo and Stitch*, or Spanish-accented Puss in Boots in DreamWorks' *Shrek 2*, as two additional examples. An interesting question arises, here, regarding how knowledge of the social location of the actors motivating the characters' voices might inform the way we (especially adults) perceive the characters, as well as how they are drawn and narrated. Our suggestion would be that while the participation of Tom Hanks certainly contributes to the heterosexuality and the whiteness of Woody, in *Toy Story*, and the voice of Will Smith contributes to the heterosexuality and the blackness of Oscar, in *Shark Tale*, this is not the only relevant (or even most significant) factor in situating the characters. Rather, it would seem more important to consider how the characters (not the actors) operate within a specific frame of reference where socialization involving race and sexuality are key. It is also significant to note that, in the end, the importance of these films resides in the fact that they are sold as mindless state-of-the-art entertainment, and not as agents of socialization. This may be the most powerful aspect of animated films for children.

4

COLONIAL CLAIMS

Indigenous People, Empire, and Naturalization

In 2008, Disney released *WALL-E*, an offbeat animated feature that centers on a robot programmed to clean up an environmentally devastated Earth several hundred years in the future. WALL-E, short for Waste Allocation Load Lifter Earth-Class, has labored in isolation since the last remnants of humanity abandoned the planet ruined by the excess of consumerism, technology, and greed. Far from a sterile machine, WALL-E displays a quirky, even lovable, personality marked by sentimentality and individuality, visible in his persistent collection of treasures amongst the trash, his enjoyment of Hollywood musicals—such as a number from *Hello, Dolly!* he replays early in the movie—and his capacity to recognize and cherish the wonder of life amid the desolation—including his pet cockroach and his recovery of a seedling.

The arrival of EVE, or Extraterrestrial Vegetative Evaluator, a robot sent from the "mother ship," in what is surely the antithesis of the Garden of Eden to which her name makes immediate reference, alters WALL-E's mundane existence when he falls instantly in love with her and returns as a stowaway to space. There, he encounters the last vestiges of humanity, a decidedly white colony dependent on technology for survival, which has at once transformed them into infantile and obese creatures who lead lives of luxury awaiting their rightful, if long delayed, return to Earth. The subsequent plot pivots around the budding romance between WALL-E and EVE, a love affair the latter resists initially, and human struggles against a supercomputer intent for them to remain in space and their own sloth to go home again. In the end, love triumphs, in the form of a figurative kiss between EVE and WALL-E that saves the day, and humanity returns to Earth, newly determined to make a foreign land, also their birthright, prosperous through hard work, perseverance, and the assistance of sophisticated technology.

Although a novel setting for animated films, *WALL-E* highlights a number of core elements of the genre, particularly with regard to its use of race, gender, and sexuality. Indeed, its appeal to the natural, the fate of humanity, the place of technology, and a future ecological disaster place it squarely in the central currents of animation in North America and the shifting contours of conversations about difference, social order, and the flows of history. Most notably for our purposes here, *WALL-E* recycles and reaffirms naturalized "facts of life": it projects gendered identities onto its robotic protagonists; it employs the idealized scripts of romantic love between a "man" and a "woman" to propel the plot; and it offers up a seeming critique of prevailing values (consumerism for instance) only to reiterate deeper "truths," including the preeminence of culture (conveyed through the trope of cultivation) and the propriety of coloniality (the claims of settler societies to the soil).

The alternative future envisioned in *WALL-E* points to the central tensions of contemporary film and summarizes our concerns in this chapter. Here, we turn to the entanglements of nature, indigenous peoples, and empire, especially as they foster ways of knowing, forms of remembrance, and means of stabilizing identities in an increasingly contested and unsettled sociohistorical conjuncture. We recognize in a series of animated features produced during the past twenty years an impulse to locate alternative readings of society, history, and the environment. On the one hand, we have seen the articulation of critical observations on the use of natural resources, suburban development, consumerism, and hunting in films like *Open Season* and *Over the Hedge* that invert or queer accepted understandings of these practices by looking at the human world from the point of view of animals (Halberstam 2008)—or at least the standpoints human animals might have of them—and the advocacy of environmentalist perspectives, such as the green philosophy animating the *Shrek* franchise (Caputi 2007). On the other hand, a decidedly anthropological gaze has refocused on indigenous peoples, conceiving of them in films such as *Brother Bear* and *Pocahontas* as having a more harmonious, highly spiritual, and thus superior relationship with the natural world (see Whitley 2008). Importantly, we read these projects, as exemplified in the films analyzed in this chapter, as largely reiterating fairly conventional assessments that invigorate prevailing categories and relations, while letting their audiences off the hook. As in *Wall-E*, nature (the natural) has long lent itself to narratives about boundaries (human:animal, technology:humanity, culture:environment), relationships, and values, while stabilizing the unspoken ideologies animating them, including race, gender, sexuality. Through the natural, animated films naturalize: they affirm common sense and taken-for-granted understandings, transforming the social, the arbitrary, and the ideological into natural facts beyond questions, outside of history, and disconnected from power.

Over the past two decades, then, as we assert in this chapter, engagements with the natural world and indigenous peoples in animated films have opened important spaces to reflect on empire in an era of intensified imperial projects, sometimes glossed as globalization and/or the New World Order, and to return to the well-worn escape routes associated with the wild—the pastoral, the savage, the virginal, the native, the natural—which has always unfolded as a symbolic and experiential space of desire, central to efforts to resolve the contradictions of history, while providing a language to name and even avoid the problems of modernity. Following Renato Rosaldo (1989), we would rightly characterize many of these projections and representations as manifestations of "imperial nostalgia," or the longing for that which one has destroyed through conquest and colonization, in this case a longing for the freedom, lifeways, values, and possibilities associated with indigeneity in the absence of indigenous peoples devastated by genocidal projects and ideological erasures.

Even after the crystallization of multiculturalism as a civil ideology, educational framework, and marketing tool, imperial nostalgia continues to shape the uses and understandings of nature and natives in animated films. Importantly, these stories, intend to acknowledge humanity and respect difference, favor the figure of the noble savage, binding the indigenous other tightly to nature as an ill-fated alter/native to and necessary pedagogic resource for EuroAmerican civilization. Of course, such renderings do not come any closer to capturing embodied Indians, their powerful cultures and histories, or the painful paths inscribed through their relations with/in the United States. The entangling of nature and native, especially in the form of a noble savage, has allowed popular culture and educational institutions to revise the stories they tell about us and them, now and then, wilderness and civilization, rewriting (if only slightly) the sincere fictions imparting fundamental elements of dominant ideologies, such as national narratives and common sense.

Our analysis contrasts movies set in Africa, *The Lion King* and *Madagascar*, and those in North America, *Pocahontas* and *Spirit*, arguing that whereas the former remove indigenous people, the latter center upon them to work through core contradictions. Our attention turns first to the timeless emptiness of Africa and then the historical fictions told about U.S. settler society. Our concluding discussion returns to the alternatives posed in these films and how they let us off the hook.

ESCAPE TO AFRICA

The sequel of the wildly successful *Madagascar* was subtitled *Escape 2 Africa*, a play on words that nicely summarizes animated films set in Africa. The so-called dark continent is an "invention" (Mazrui 2005; Mudimbe 1988). A rich source of natural resources and inexhaustible resource for imperial imaginings, it has served as a heterotopia, another space in which Europeans and Americans have elaborated fantasies about savagery, wildness, and the state of nature. Media persist in picturing it as a place apart, an inhuman setting marked by violence, abject suffering, backwardness, and chaos. Indeed, according to James Michira (2002), several themes dominate conversations about Africa in the West: homogeneity, wildness, feminine, endemic conflict, political instability, and HIV/AIDS. These themes induce indifference, pity, and revulsion, encouraging many Europeans and Americans to turn away from Africa and Africans. In contrast, even as they have returned to and re-invented Africa, animated films have mapped out ideological excursions that project fantasies upon it. And while they do not, and arguably cannot given their audience, dwell on the dehumanizing elements of prevailing discourse, they do in fact reiterate its fundamental grammar: *The Lion King*, *Madagascar* and its sequel, and *Tarzan* all take audiences to an imagined Africa—a vacant, timeless, malleable setting to restate social facts in a natural register.

The Africa projected through these films is utopian. It is no place, with the exception of the first installment of the *Madagascar* franchise, which only makes general references to the massive eponymous island, the famed lemurs, and the autochthonous fossa; the settings of the others remains unspecified, generic—the rain forest, the prideland, the savannah. Moreover, the homogeneity of the continent is confirmed through the timeless and/or ahistorical elements of the narratives. Whereas *The Lion King* is set in a world outside of the flow of time, *Tarzan* appears to be generically historical, perhaps best phrased as Victorian, and the pair of *Madagascar* films play out in a kind of untethered now in which history and context have no place. In all four of these films, the surface action takes precedence, anchored by the flows of the life cycle, the turning of the seasons, "the circle of life," and/or the flow of tradition. In a very real way, they each deploy an ethnographic present to offer fantastic narratives which might be said to be utopian, that is a moral aspiration and didactic imaging set in a nowhere.

Africa may be the only place pictured in animated films that has no human occupants. In none of these films can one find an indigenous community or local person. No one has a claim to this locality; there is no need to mention the legacies of colonialism or the imprint of underdevelopment. Empty places, devoid of humanity, the ideal screen for Hollywood projections. As Chinua Achebe (1977, 788) noted in his reflections on Joseph Conrad:

Africa as setting and backdrop which eliminates the African as human factor. Africa as a metaphysical battlefield devoid of all recognizable humanity, into which the wandering European enters at his peril. Of course, there is a preposterous and perverse kind of arrogance in thus reducing Africa to the role of props for the breakup of one petty European mind. But that is not even the point. The real question is the dehumanization of Africa and Africans which this age-long attitude has fostered and continues to foster in the world.

The erasure of Africans is a violent act, a symbolic clearing. A measure of the significance can be glimpsed in the people placed on this stage. Upon leaving New York, the animals in *Madagascar* only have one further encounter with humans, and that in the form of skeleton in the wreckage of a plane—the remnant of an outsider consumed by the hostile environment. In the sequel, poachers threaten life on the reserve and tourists go on safari. Importantly, the only possible African in the movie, who leads the tourists, does not have the skills to survive in the rain forest and defers leadership to an elderly, if scrappy, woman from New York. Similarly, in *Tarzan*, whites, Europeans, foreign to Africa, are the only human agents. The title character is of the British ruling class, who tragically loses his family to the dark continent and lives among the wild animals of "the jungle" until encountering Jane and the expedition she has accompanied to Africa.

Importantly, in the absence of embodied natives, the children of nature, the animals, stand in for/as them. Not unlike the recent I Am Africa campaign, in which celebrities, including Gwyneth Paltrow and David Bowie, adorned with "tribal" elements such as face paint, proclaimed a connection to the continent in an effort to raise awareness of it, the animal protagonists of animated films set in Africa go native or, better said, play at being Africans in a manner recognizable to their audiences. Organized into something resembling "tribes," within or across species boundaries, they consult "witch doctors," modify their bodies with paint, feathers, and vegetation, engage in traditional rituals—to affirm manhood and participation in the community—and have world-views marked by superstition and animism. Interestingly, those outside of the tribe do not resemble stereotypes of Africans; rather they draw upon the U.S. language of racialized social problems. In *The Lion King*, for instance, the darkness beyond the prideland, marked by the elephant graveyard and prowled by the hyenas, is an allegory for urban America:

> First, it uses Whoopi Goldberg's and Cheech Marin's voices to represent the speech of two of three prominent hyena characters as black English and Latino slang, respectively. Second, it depicts the building that is the hyena's abode as a bleak-looking and over-crowded high-rise, the unambiguous image of a housing development in the projects. (Gooding-Williams 2006, 38)

Clearly, the audience is meant to identify with the animals, who play at being native, and recognize the threat to the natural order in the form of more familiar and troubling outsiders. Manuel M. Martin-Rodriguez (2000) pushes this argument to its logical conclusion, asserting that *The Lion King*, far from being an innocent adaptation of folklore or even *Hamlet* (Buhler 2003), is better read as an effort to engage and work through the competition and conflict associated with Latino migration northward, an allegory that restabilizes the white core through a story about lions and hyenas in an invented Africa.

As the social world finds expression through nature in these movies, it is naturalized. While we glimpse this in the hyenas in *The Lion King*, it gains expression across all of these films as natural hierarchies reflect and reinforce social stratification. Where *Madagascar*, through Alex the lion's struggles with his carnivorous instinct, both levels distinction among species and shows the chaos resulting from the denial of programmed desires, its sequel and *The Lion King* present a natural ranking of species, in which lions rightly rule as masters of the land. They ascribe, as Gooding-Williams (2006) reminds us, to a Hegelian framework, insisting on a great chain of being that places everyone in discernible and discrete hierarchal location. These are not mere reflections of nature, but as Martin-Rodriguez and Gooding-Williams assert, they crystallize as racial allegories, endowing whites with superiority. Importantly, *Tarzan* takes this motif even further, clearly articulating a vision of white supremacy, little changed from the heights of Jim Crow racism and the white man's burden.

Animated features set in Africa have allowed filmmakers and their audiences the privilege of taking and remaking Africa. It has granted them the capacity to poach practices and artifacts and project fears and fantasies. Carrying the imperial logic of erasure and assimilation at its extreme, they simultaneously reinforce notions of exotic difference and vanish Africans, clearing the generic time-space thus created for a recolonization by Eurocentric projections and preoccupations. Although the color line has famously faded, it appears to still shine brightly in animated invigorations of the dark continent.

THE POLITICS OF INCLUSION

In a sense, *The Lion King*, the *Madagascar* franchise, and *Tarzan* allow their consumers to escape (to) Africa, enjoying pleasurable diversion as they avoid the burdens of (neo)imperialism and its impacts. In contrast, animated features about natives and nature set in North America hinge on encounters with different people and practices, which derive an equally rich history of invention (Berkhofer 1979), take place in more specific contexts, attend to culture, and work through unresolved issues in the contemporary. While *Brother Bear* spins a fairly formulaic morality tale set in the sub-Arctic at the end of the Ice Age, it portends a certain sensitivity and affirms a fascination with the ecological Indian before the Fall (Krech 2000). Meant to convey a deeper truth about coming of age, developing humility, and respecting nature, it also provides an occasion for American audiences to engage environmental concerns through an archetypal portal. This portal of course is constructed to the specification of contemporary EuroAmericans and has only the loosest of connections to the Paleolithic.

Pocahontas, the subject of much critical attention (see Aidman 1999; Amici 2007; Dundes 2001; Giese 1996; Parekh 2003; Sardar 2002; Strong 1996) and discussed at some length in the introduction, makes a similar move: the noble savage in harmony with the natural world, clearing a space for reflection on an alternate (and largely imagined) environmentalism. In common with the 2003 release, it stresses the metaphysical relationship between native and nature, complete with animal sidekicks and talking trees. More important, however, *Pocahontas* is a national narrative: it is a story about how America came into being and a commentary on race relations at the turn of millennium.

Pocahontas is one of the clearest statements of post-racial consciousness produced in the 1990s. The film acknowledges that bad things happened in the past, worthy of lament and perhaps even regret. Everyone knows the outcome. In spite of this pending and palpable tragedy, it suggests not that racism, imperialism, or other articulations of ideological frames and material conditions matter, but that everyone is ethnocentric, has the capacity to be prejudiced, and may be pressed to irrationality and violence. The mutual misrecognition at the core of the film is given the clearest expression in the song cycles, "Savages." The Powhatan sing: "They're different from us. Which means they can't be trusted. We must sound the drums of war. They're savages! Savages!" And the colonists respond, "They're not like you and me. Which means they must be evil. We must sound the

drums of war! They're savages! Savages! Dirty redskin devils!"
Understood in context, of course, these phrases or the utterance
have no equivalence, but *Pocahontas* works mightily to erase
racism and its connection to settler colonialism. It proposes human nature as the seat of the problem and the only solution. For
love conquers all here and Pocahontas emerges as a kind of mediator, bridging the gap between settler and native, civilization
and nature, through her heterosexual desire for Captain Smith.
This union and sacrifice marks in many respects the beginning of
America qua a settler state. Importantly, *Pocahontas* in refusing
history in favor of universal humanism and romance over and
against power gives its viewers an important way out in which they
incorporate the other, literally allowing them to lay claim to land
through Pocahontas and cross-cultural borderlands via love. Coloniality erased and affirmed in one subtle gesture.

An arguably more complex rendering of the entanglements of
indigeneity and environment can be found in *Spirit*. In the subsequent section, we read it in some detail to tease out the articulations of (dis)placement and (dis)identification.

Redrawing the Frontier

Spirit, a beautifully drawn feature from DreamWorks Entertainment, tells the story of a wild Kiger mustang born free in the
American West in the late nineteenth century, who, following his
capture by the U.S. Cavalry, must struggle to regain his independence and return to his herd. The movie places horses at its center, using their actions and relationships to make broader lessons
about nature, freedom, and civilization meaningful. In addition to
the protagonist and narrator, Spirit (Matt Damon), two other
horses figure prominently, his mother and Rain, a paint he encounters and whom he comes to love. People, in turn, play a more
marginal role. In fact, only two men emerge from the background

to shape the dramatic events of the stallion's life, the brash and stern Colonel (James Cromwell) and the young and caring Lakota Little Creek (Daniel Studi). Importantly, unlike many movies aimed at children, while Spirit has a voice and narrates the story, neither he nor the other animals actually speak to one another or the human characters. Moreover, in contrast with most Westerns, the equine is not cast as an instrument of conquest and domesticated or subservient, but instead is the central force of the narrative, a persistent sign of liberty.

Spirit opens with the birth of its mustang hero, painting his coming of age through the bold movement of the herd across the lush, boundless plains and valleys of the West and brief scenes in which the curiosity and spunk of the young stallion seemingly court trouble, only to find comedic resolution. Spirit, like his father before him, matures into the leader of his herd, evidenced not simply by his obvious power, strength, and majesty as he moves across the screen, but more obviously through his fearless defense of two young foals threatened by a cougar. The Cimarron herd, happy and free, lives in peace and harmony with the world around it, until, one day, something new comes to the land, people. The intrusion of a group of cowboys, introduced as little more than a campfire on the horizon, piques the curiosity of Spirit, who, despite his mother's efforts, takes it upon himself to investigate. The mustang stallion, now reproached by the domesticated horses of the strangers, cautiously explores the campsite, getting his first glimpse of the odd ways of what he calls the two-legged, including strange clothing, foul-tasting liquor, and fire. His inquiry awakens the camp and a chase ensues, which quickly changes from a playful display of Spirit's bravado to a fierce effort to escape. Spirit leads the cowboys away from his herd and is eventually caught, brought under control by several of his pursuers.

Once ensnared, he is marched away from his lush homeland, across a barren landscape to a fort. Here, the Colonel instructs his troops to induct Spirit. Unbroken despite his capture, Spirit vigorously resists the efforts of soldiers, head-butting, kicking, and biting as his handlers cut his mane, attempt to shoe him, and endeavor to brand him. The uproarious scene, which leaves the blacksmith unconscious and all the other horses in stables laughing, transforms the escalating struggle between man and beast into a humorous statement of the obvious: man cannot (and should not try to) tame the wild. Undeterred, the Colonel next orders his soldiers to break Spirit. In turn, they unsuccessfully try to ride the wild mustang; all meet the same fate, being thrown, but each in a unique and more amusing fashion. Determined to break Spirit, the cavalry officer has the stallion tied to a post in the middle of the corral for three days without food or water. The cruelty of this strategy is underscored and personalized when at the peak of the second day's heat, the Colonel, making eye contact with an envious and angry Spirit, drinks cool water, splashing the remainder on his face and neck.

On the second day, the soldiers capture "a hostile," who we later learn is named Little Creek. The Colonel immediately recognizes him as a Lakota, suggesting this must be the case because he lacks the fine features of the Crow and the stature of the Cheyenne. He orders that he too be tied to a post in the middle of the fort. At daybreak on the third day, Little Creek communicates through animal calls with unseen others outside the fort who successfully toss a knife just within the young warrior's reach. Able to free himself, but unable to escape because of revelry, Little Creek must bide his time. He watches as the Colonel himself attempts to break Spirit, an intensely choreographed scene in which each exerts his will with ferocious intensity. In the end, it appears that the cavalry officer has prevailed and he offers a grand speech about progress, civilization, and manifest destiny. In his words:

> You see, gentlemen, any horse can be broken. . . . There are those in Washington who believe the West will never be settled, the Northern Pacific Railroad will never reach Nebraska, a hostile Lakota will never submit to Providence and it is that manner of small thinking that would say this horse could never be broken. Discipline, time, and patience are the three great levelers.

At the close, Spirit throws the Colonel, who reaches for a rifle with which to shoot the beast. In the nick of time, Little Creek intercedes, mounting the stallion and dislodging the weapon just as the Colonel pulls the trigger. The pair romp through the stables, freeing the other horses, all of whom are the same dark brown, in contrast with Spirit's golden hue, before escaping from the fort.

Spirit, who thinks he has regained his freedom and soon will return to his herd, is sadly disappointed when Little Creek, upon reuniting with his friends outside the fort, places a rope around his neck and leads him toward his village. In a pristine river valley, the stallion again enters a corral and those around him seek to break him. Once more hilarity accompanies human efforts to tame the wild mustang. Resolute in his desire to make Spirit his own, Little Creek gently and compassionately endeavors to domesticate him. Central to this kinder and gentler approach is Rain, a paint mare ridden throughout the film by Little Creek. The Lakota warrior ties the two horses together with a long piece of rope, leaving them to their own devices. Spirit tries to escape but Rain resists, causing the former to think of the latter as a traitor to her kind. With time, the two fall in love. And Little Creek comes to appreciate Spirit as a friend. In the end, Little Creek concludes that no one will ever ride Spirit, nor should they, and he releases the stallion.

Free at last, Spirit endeavors to convince Rain to run away with him. Before she can make up her mind, the U.S. Cavalry descends on the village. Under the leadership of the unnamed Colonel, undoubtedly modeled after the notorious George A. Custer, the cavalry attacks the peaceful Lakota community. In the conflict that follows, Rain is shot and washed down the river, followed by Spirit, who rushes to save his love. The mustang succeeds in pulling her from the water, but fears Rain will die, as he is taken as a trophy by the soldiers after the battle.

Captured once more, Spirit is placed on a railroad car. As he heads west, the landscape again turns barren and snow begins to fall. Little Creek sets out on foot after his friend. Arriving at a base camp, Spirit and the other horses are pressed into work hauling a massive train engine over a mountain pass. As they near the crest, Spirit realizes that the railroad line being built is headed right for his homeland and will ultimately destroy it. Resisting the march of progress, he feigns death. As he is drug away from the teams of horses, he escapes and works to free the other horses. In turn, the massive locomotive slides back down the mountainside, chasing Spirit and carving a path of destruction in its wake. At the foot of the mountain, it hurtles into the base camp, causing an explosion and fire that rapidly engulfs the forest and threatens to kill Spirit.

Happily, Little Creek saves the day and leads the stallion away from the fire, coming face-to-face with his nemesis, the Colonel. The cavalry officer and a group of soldiers give chase, pursuing the pair of friends up a butte. At the summit, there appears to be no way out, save for an impossible jump. With the soldiers rapidly closing in, Spirit gallops to the edge of the butte and springs into the air; after a slow motion flight across the gap, the two land in a heap, but still find the guns of the cavalry pointed at them. Impressed with the tenacity and power of the mustang, the Colonel orders his troops to stand down.

Finally free, Spirit reunites with Rain. The two horses return to the Cimarron herd. Once more in the wild, they live happily ever after.

UNBROKEN IDEOLOGIES

Spirit is much more than an entertaining film aimed at children. It is a powerful statement about nature, history, culture, and their relationships. Indeed, it exemplifies popular environmentalist discourse: on the one hand, it formulates a pronounced critique of modern life, particularly its attitudes toward nature; on the other hand, its use of natural symbols and indigenous imagery reaffirms values and ideals central to contemporary systems of environmental, social, and racial injustice.

Breaking a Mustang

Arguably the key moment in the film is the struggle to break Spirit. To be sure, this scene reinforces Elizabeth Lawrence's (1985) observation that such conflicts between man and stallion invariably are tests of manhood. What's more, this battle in *Spirit* pits two versions of masculinity against one another. The Colonel represents the rationalized masculinity of a trained soldier and of a promise keeper of modern civilization, a masculinity marked by control, precision, persistence, and willpower. In contrast, Spirit embodies the natural man; more primal, more authentic, he demands, defies authority, rises to affronts from others, and aggressively asserts himself regardless of the dangers or consequences, which is why he and Little Creek were both tied to a post at some point. Within the film, stallion and Indian represent the same: the wild that needed taming by the civilizing force of the cavalry. Importantly, Spirit's ultimate triumph underscores the victory of wildness over civilization central to the film. Beyond the powerful entanglements of gender and nature, efforts to break Spirit also highlight a deep desire at the heart of the movie. Not unlike indigenous people, then and now, horses, according to Jane Tompkins (1992, 93), "express a need for connection to nature, to the wild . . . [they] fulfill a longing for a different *kind* of existence. Antimodern, antiurban, and antitechnological, they stand for an existence without cars and telephones and electricity."

A Moralized Landscape

Spirit renders the world in stark, reductive contrasts. In part, this may be a function of what wild mustangs have signified in American culture; in the words of Elizabeth Lawrence (1985), a beast typically bound and domesticated remains free, unifying a set of fundamental contradictions: wild/tame, free/captive, savagery/ civilization. More significantly, in this case, it is not simply that the film pivots around a series of binary oppositions, which it does, but that it links the categorical distinctions together to encode larger metanarratives. For instance:

U.S. Fort/Indian Village
Railroad/Cimarron Herd Homeland
Civilization/Nature
White/Red
Bondage/Freedom
Domestication/Wilderness
Modern/Primitive
Change/Transcendence
Desert/River Valley
Terror/Love
Harsh/Nurturing
Bleak/Lush

Together, these symbolic juxtapositions form what Roland Barthes would term myths, naturalized accounts of the world that individuals take for granted as true. In *Spirit*, modern life, or civilization, represented in the Colonel, the military outpost in the desert, and the railroad built in winter, is cold and bleak; it embodies the destruction of the wilderness, of individuality, of difference; it cultivates discipline, control, and restraint; it stresses domination, assimilation, and means over ends. In contrast, nature, embodied by Spirit and Little Creek, is bright and bountiful; it demands interdependence, particularly friendship and love; it fosters independence, liberty, and individuality; it is uncontrollable. *Spirit* communicates these messages not simply because it is an animated feature or a movie aimed at children. Rather, these metanarratives, no less than the categorical distinctions underlying them, inform a commonsense understanding of social problems and environmental issues. Their centrality to *Spirit* points attention to the mythic structures at the heart of popular notions of the American West, explaining how "we" came to be, a not-so-happy ending of the triumph of civilization, the successful completion of the railroad, and the claiming of the land from natives and nature alike, reglossed in the film in a manner that allows viewers to distance themselves from these acts and enjoy the privileges accorded by them.

A Confused Geography

Spirit takes place in the American West, itself the subject of much moralizing and mythmaking. In contrast with the symbolic meanings of the wild mustang refusing to be broken and the metanarrative of wildness/civilization, the mapping of the West in *Spirit* works to reinforce commonsense understandings of nation, history, and place (Mitchell 2003).

The film opens with a bald eagle soaring, following its flight through the Grand Canyon north toward Arches National Monument and eventually to the forested valleys and mountains of Glacier National Park. Immense, beautiful, and mythic, the landscape is not anonymous. Rather, it is a collection of recognizable natural wonders that are also considered national treasures. In a sense, the mythic map inscribed in the film permits a kind of claiming and forgetting. Audiences know and recognize these places, bounded sites of wilderness carved out from the surrounding landscape that all viewers will identify as part of the United States and its heritage. Moreover, the odd condensation of the desert and the mountains, the slippage between the location of the fort and the Lakota village, and the very presence of a Lakota in what appears to be the desert southwest further underscore the confused spatial imagination of the film. Linking these natural/national locations together encourages audiences to misunderstand the West, erase its indigenous inhabitants, and construct a historical geography by weaving together a fanciful rendering of the region with mappings of the present.

Natural History

Spirit offers an equally troubling account of history. The cultural conflicts arising from EuroAmerican imperialism and expansion form the backdrop for the film. And to be sure, *Spirit* does not celebrate the conquest of Native America, but its rendering of the past does reinforce the amnesia and privileges associated with white supremacy in the present.

To begin, the film misplaces indigeneity. Spirit and his herd are introduced as the natural and native residents of the West. In his narrative, the mustang uses language often associated with American Indian storytelling. For instance, Spirit refers to people as the two-legged, and he speaks of them as foreigners, strangers, and new. Indeed, the world of the Cimarron herd falls out of balance with the arrival of something new in the land. Converting an imported species into natives trivializes the claims and conditions of actual indigenous peoples.

Furthermore, *Spirit* refuses to comment on consequences for indigenous peoples. During the framing narrative of the film, Spirit remarks that his story records important events, but he will leave it to the viewer to decide what happened, who was right, and who was wrong.

> The story I want to tell you cannot be found in a book. They say the history of the West was written from the saddle of a horse, but it's never been told from the heart of one, not 'til now. I was born here in this place that came to be called the Old West, but to my kind the land was ageless. It had no beginning and no end—no boundary between earth and sky. Like the wind in the buffalo grass we belonged here. We would always belong here. They say the mustang is the spirit of the West. Whether that West was won or lost in the end you'll have to decide for yourself, but the story I want to tell you is true. I was there, and I remember.

Consequently, it completely disavows the articulations of truth and power in either past events or their contemporary retellings.

Even when the pain of the past intrudes, the movie cannot bring itself to address the significance of its story. On one occasion, the Colonel and his troops raid a Lakota village. This event, reminiscent of tragic attacks at Sand Creek, Washita, and Wounded Knee, completely lacks context. What provoked it? What is the broader conflict? What might the indigenous actors say? What is the outcome? How many were killed, injured, and left homeless? Answering such queries, let alone depicting them, would have meant suggesting that history was something other than a backdrop, an objective record, a natural chain of events.

The film individualizes historical processes and social struggles, condensing them around the three main characters: the Colonel, Little Creek, and Spirit. Personality, not structures or power, disperses questions about the past. Individuals make history, they make mistakes, they can be evil, they can do bad things.

CONCLUSION

In many ways, the myths energizing *Spirit* do not educate viewers as much as they miseducate them, distorting race, history, and power. At the same time they reinforce well-known historical narratives involving manifest destiny and a right to land. These distortions derive from both the content and the form of the film. *Spirit* encourages its audience to identify with the stallion and entertain, if not accept, his traumatic interactions as an indictment of the evils of civilization, while letting "settlers" off the hook as the benefactors of modernity and arguably the enactors of its force fields in the present. At the same time, identifying with Spirit naturalizes the proposed differences between EuroAmericans and Native Americans, while rendering their demise as an inevitable and organic process, relieving viewers of an accountability for its legacies (we take on this point again in the next chapter in relation to animated portrayals of indigenous societies in the Americas). Consequently, *Spirit* pivots around its longing for lost worlds, its desire for those natural forms and native cultural forms destroyed by civilization and conquest. Viewers may grieve, even feel guilty, but they need not be situated in relation to social structures or historical flows in any meaningful way. They need only to revel in natural beauty (which remains to this day), marveling at its native features (including indigenous peoples), and in the end lament the suffering and struggle associated with their decimation. And as Spirit tells them, it is for them to decide whether the West was won or lost; that is to say, it is for them to decide whether such decimation was worth it or not. Reflecting deeper trends with recent racialized narratives for children and multiculturalism more generally imperial nostalgia for native and nature, then, paces *Spirit* in two distinct ways. On the one hand, (racial and cultural) difference clears a space to differentiate past and present, grounding powerful critiques of historic commitments to racism, progress, and domination, even as it veils recent reformulations. On the other hand, the longing for the lost and destroyed oddly fosters a kind of amnesia in which the passing of once-proud people is an object of esteem and yearning, while the processes, relations, and ideologies remain invisible.

5

OTHER(ED) LATINIDADES

Animated Representations of (Latino) Ethnicity and Nation

Released in 2006, *Happy Feet* became the 2007 Oscar winner for Best Animated Feature Film. Immersing the audience into a fantastic world of emperor penguins, on a broader level the story warns us of the dangerous touch humans can have on nature and natural resources and narrates the epic adventures of Mumble, a different kind of emperor penguin who, though an outcast, tries to save his "people" from humans (who are fittingly called "aliens" by the Arctic fauna). Similar to other animated films, to develop Mumble's quest, *Happy Feet* relies on mainstream sexual(ized) and racial(ized) notions. The film begins with a narrator telling the audience that his parents met the usual way (singing) and "the song became love, and love became the egg." From the moment he was born, Mumble had to fight to belong in the world of emperor penguins, where "a penguin without a heart song is hardly a penguin at all." Mumble did not have a song; he had his feet, which were in constant rhythmic movement. It was this combination of no song and "weird feet" that rendered him an outcast. In a move that can be considered pretty progressive, the film also shows the danger of "staying the course" without allowing room for organic social change. This is best exemplified by the rift between the elders and Mumble, when he tries to tell his community that food is scarce because of the "aliens."

Happy Feet also provides audiences with less progressive racial messages, as the film utilizes problematic racialized constructions to move the plot along. When Mumble is struggling to fit in, he meets a group of short penguins with Chicano vato accents and Spanish names (Rinaldo, Lombardo, Ramon, Raul, and Nestor) who become his friends and call him "Tall Boy." The short penguins, who sprinkle Spanish here and there in their conversations, call themselves "the amigos" and live in a community where penguins seem to live in a constant state of fiesta. The amigos, of course, convince Mumble to "cheat" and pretend he is singing a Spanish rendition of "My Way" to Gloria, the love of his life (Ramon is actually doing the singing). Gloria of course discovers the fraud, and Mumble decides to convince her that there are other ways in which they can complement each other, as he tries to dance to her song. The other young emperor penguins along with the amigos join the dance/singing party, creating an environment that the elders feel is objectionable, calling it "uprising, unruly nonsense." One of the elders finally puts a stop to it and the following exchange takes place:

> Elder: A little self-control, if you please. You bring this disorder, this aberration to the very heart of our community. Have you lost your minds? It is this kind of backsliding that has brought this scarcity upon us.
>
> Raul: Um, excuse me, smiley. Can you speak plain penguin, please?

Mumble: He thinks the food shortage has something to do with me.

Elder: Can you not understand that we can only survive here when we're in harmony? When you and your foreign friends lead us into your easy ways, you offend the Great 'Guin.

The elders calling the "Latino" penguins foreign, even though they also belong to the Arctic, and talking about their ways as "easy" are clear reproductions of current interpretations of immigration in the United States. The way in which the exchange unfolds can be interpreted as a subtle critique of racism and xenophobia as it takes place in the United States. But, by putting that language and those ideas on the beaks of the elders, *Happy Feet* seems to suggest that racism and xenophobia among emperor penguins, just as in the United States, are a thing of the (dying or already dead) past. The overt images of the happy, always dancing, worry-free, and heavily accented penguins, however, seem to overwhelm any subtle messages the film is trying to convey.

The anthropomorphized representations of Latino penguins in *Happy Feet* fit and add to a steady stream of Latino characters in animated films, which seemed to increase significantly after the 1990s, when the United States produced what some scholars have dubbed the "Latino boom" in popular culture (Berg 2002; Lugo-Lugo 2004). The "boom" included an unprecedented number of Latino/a celebrities (mainly singers, actors, and athletes) at the center of U.S. mainstream popular culture, and a relentless consumption of various aspects of "Latino" cultures. We could only sit back and watch as Mexican salsa reached number one status as a condiment, as Puerto Rican salsa music reached ballroom dance status, as J.Lo and Ricky Martin became sensations by shaking their bonbons, and as the racialized bodies of Salma Hayek and Christina Aguilera made it to national celebrity headlines. Indeed, mainstream American culture seemed to develop a taste for all things "Latino," as Corona Extra became, in 1997, the number one imported beer in the United States, replacing Heineken for the first time (mind-advertising.com). Thus, the commodification and mainstreaming of Latinos/as, Latino/a cultures, and Latino/a bodies during the last decade of the twentieth century seemed not only merciless but also inescapable.

It was also during the 1990s (and perhaps as a response to and extension of the happenings in popular culture) that political pundits in the United States began to discuss the effects of a sizable and ever-increasing Latino population. The 1990 census showed that 9 percent of the U.S. population (22,354,059 individuals) could trace their heritage back to a Latin American country or Spain, and by 2000, 12.5 percent (35,305,818 individuals) claimed to be of Hispanic/Latino origin. In fact, after the statistics of the 2000 Census were released, it was predicted that by the year 2050, Latinos would be the largest minority in the United States. Politicians began to discuss the "Latino" block in elections, and for the first time in U.S. history, both presidential candidates in 2000 delivered speeches (or part of speeches) in Spanish. Corporate executives became fully aware of the situation and seemed to discover that Latinos were also a powerful consumer force. Thus, some companies began to release products that mainstreamed Latino cultures (for instance Frito Lay released Guacamole Doritos, Salsa Doritos, and Salsa Verde Doritos), while others began to attract Latino consumers by consistently advertising their products in Spanish and/or in Spanish-speaking venues (consider, for instance, back issues of *Latina* magazine from the last decade or so).

During this most recent "discovery" of Latinos by mainstream America, several images surrounding their "attributes" were reified: their brownness, their hotness, and, most certainly, their exotic "nature," that is to say, their otherness. These attributes/

images have been mostly (re)created by the machinery that is popular culture. As Feagin, Vera, and Batur (2001, 193) convey about African Americans, "[m]uch of what Whites know today about African Americans comes from the media." This argument can be extended to other racialized groups, including, of course, Latinos, for in the 1990s, the media not only rediscovered, but also re-invented Latinos.

It is our argument in this chapter that the Latino boom witnessed in the 1990s spilled into the world of animation in 2000, when both DreamWorks and Disney released two animated films emerging from the Latino craze in the broader society: *The Road to El Dorado* and *The Emperor's New Groove*. Even though they were set in places other than the United States (*El Dorado* was set in a mythical land in the "new world" on the verge of its conquest, and *New Groove* was set in the pre-conquest South American Andes), both films teach lessons about Latinos in the United States, as well as about the relationship between Latinoness and whiteness. Similar to contemporary animated films covering "historical periods" in the United States (for example, Disney's *Pocahontas* and DreamWorks' *Spirit*), these films can be seen as "a rewrite of history that bleaches colonialism of its genocidal legacy" (Giroux 1999, 101). This chapter examines the ways in which these animated films echo the broader society in their articulations of history by erasing the brutality of certain events (such as the conquest), and by juxtaposing images that are usually associated with "Latinoness" in the United States against images of whiteness.

In his book *Racist America*, Joe Feagin (2001) identifies ten ways in which contemporary America develops and perpetuates a racist ideology. Four of those are particularly relevant to the two films we will discuss in this chapter:

(1) *Asserting innocence, denying racism*—this way of looking at history emphasizes that the United States has developed a

rosy view of history, constantly foregrounding the notion of white innocence;

(2) *Sincere fictions of the white self: romanticizing the past*—this particular way of looking at history works in conjunction with the previous element and centers the role of whiteness, portraying whites as generous and kind;

(3) *A whitewashed worldview*—this aspect includes "all the mental images, prejudiced attitudes, stereotypes, fictions, racist explanations, and rationalizations that link to systemic racism and make up a white racist worldview, one deeply imbedded in the dominant culture and institutions" (99); and

(4) *Fear of a multiracial, multicultural future*—a multiracial and a multicultural society is perceived as a direct threat to white supremacy.

We will use these four components of a racist ideology in the contemporary United States described by Feagin to develop our discussion of *El Dorado* and *New Groove*. In addition, we will use Annalee Ward's (2002) description of Disney's animated films as storytellers, and as "central . . . communicator[s] in contemporary life," given that as she points out, they are "many of the first narratives children use to learn about the world" (1). These narratives are so powerful, she tells us, that they have been able to evolve "over time, adapting to cultural changes" (113) and are able to "communicate arguments for a moral life or an immoral one" (114). In the case of Disney films, she maintains, each individual film is a chapter in "the Disney book" that teaches what "the world looks like or what it ought to look like" (116). Thus, the full body of Disney films represents a very distinct worldview, and can be seen as propaganda that asserts and reinforces whiteness as a supremacist ideology. As discussed in our introduction, we argue that when it comes to animated films, the analyses scholars have offered vis-à-vis Disney can be extended to other animated films. This case is no exception, for Ward's discussion applies to both *Emperor's New Groove* (which is a Disney movie) and *The Road to El Dorado* (which is not a Disney movie).

Although these two films are not, at face value, about American history, they do focus on historical events that have been folded into the national narrative of how the country came to be the United States of America. The combination of half-truths and whole misrepresentations (that is, "sincere fictions") has created a whitewashed world in which whiteness is innocent and noble, and non-whiteness is innocent and childlike (at best) or innocent and mischievous (at worst). In the words of Giroux (1999, 30), this recasting of history is particularly relevant, for it has given "new meaning to the politics of innocence, and has provided a narrative for shaping public memory and for producing a 'general body of identifications' that promote a sanitized version of American history." This sanitized version of history is at the core of the films discussed in this chapter, both of which show overt attempts at shaping audience memories about the Americas both before and during the conquest. As part of the sanitation efforts and shaping of public memories, the "history" we see represented in these films overlooks any oppressive elements that have maintained racialized, non-white groups in the margins (such as genocide, stealing of lands, rape, and slavery) centuries after the conquest and colonization began. In particular, the narratives of "discovery" and "conquest" have served as sanitized preambles and as complementary aspects to the narrative of manifest destiny. This is why our students are able to say (without blinking) that "Christopher Columbus discovered America [meaning the United States] and that, as a result, people of European descent deserve to be here [meaning the Americas]." These "sincere fictions" have created a "whitewashed world" within the context of the United States, where strategic aspects of the history of the Americas is transformed into and recast as U.S. history.

THE ROAD TO LATINAJE: *EL DORADO*, EXOTIC OTHERS, AND NATURAL-BORN LEADERS

Although a DreamWorks production, *The Road to El Dorado* uses a similar formula to that used by Disney, which as Feagin (2001) and Giroux (1999) point out, includes the portrayal of whiteness as innocence, and a promising and hopeful account of history. In addition, as we discussed in chapter 1, although *El Dorado* conforms to Disney's worldview of classic structures and dichotomies about good and evil, as a "central communicator" the film also constructs an after-the-fact morality that teaches us what the conquest "really" looked like. By including romantic representations of history and historical events, the film portrays a past that is devoid of any negative connotations, including a consistent, across-time representation of whites "as powerful, brave, cordial, kind, firm, good-looking, and generous: a[s] natural-born leader[s]" (Feagin 2001, 98). Specifically, *El Dorado* constructs images of whites as natural-born leaders in the form of a collage of attributes embodied by three of the main (white) characters: Hernán Cortez (who, though portrayed in a negative light in the film, is still depicted as powerful, brave, and firm—three of the qualities listed by Feagin), and Tulio and Miguel (who are portrayed as cordial, kind, good-looking, and generous—the rest of the qualities listed by him).

In essence, *El Dorado* can be seen as a contributor to the Disney "propaganda" trying to present the conquest in a light similar to that of mainstream history: as a wonderful event that gave birth to us, to modern society, to our civilization. It is in this particular portrayal that history is rewritten, and whiteness is articulated as an innocent (by)product of that history. For instance, we learn from the beginning that even though Tulio and Miguel are con artists, they actually arrive in the Americas as stowaways after a series of unfortunate and fortuitous circumstances. Thus, they are not gold diggers, they are not conquerors, but they are innocent [white] men "dealing" with the situation (the situation of arriving in El Dorado by mistake) the best they can. In addition, once in the Americas (in what is now Mexico, we must presume), these best friends are mistaken for and treated as gods. The most interesting feature of Tulio's and Miguel's characters is that, flaws notwithstanding, they are able to save the indigenous culture from itself and from Cortez. Thus, within this context, brownness exists because whiteness allows it to exist by helping it to survive. In fact, in El Dorado, the whiteness of Tulio and Miguel is galvanized by the brownness of the other characters. Tulio and Miguel can be cordial, kind, good-looking, and ultimately generous (the images of natural-born leaders they embody) because the brown characters are not (at least not naturally so). We will use three of the main "brown" characters to illustrate this point: Tzekel-Kan (the high priest), Tannabok (the chief), and Chel (the "girl").

Tzekel-Kan is the only unconditionally mean "brown character," and though similar to the character of Cortez, there are some key differences between the two. For instance, while Cortez's negative figure resides in the background during most of the story, Tzekel-Kan's figure appears immediately upon the arrival of Tulio and Miguel in El Dorado. This makes Tulio and Miguel more vulnerable to Tzekel-Kan's meanness. Tzekel-Kan's malevolence is such that he plots against his own people. In fact, he commits the ultimate betrayal by trying to lead Cortez to El Dorado, a place that his people had tried to maintain hidden for generations. Although it could be argued that Tzekel-Kan's character is as mean and unredeemable as Cortez's, Tzekel-Kan is committing a bigger offense by conning his own people and, thus, he receives the harshest punishment in the film: he becomes Cortez's slave. In the case of Cortez, the punishment for his "meanness" is less severe: he was just not able to find El Dorado. However, at the end of the film, as it becomes evident that El Dorado is out of reach for Cortez, he and his escort continue walking deeper inland, and we are reminded of the historical facts: in the end, and in spite of not finding the people of El Dorado, Cortez was rewarded for his qualities as a natural-born leader, as he was able to plunder the lands and colonize the peoples of what we now know as Mexico. What is most troubling about these two differential "punishments" is that in the case of Cortez, his punishment (not being able to locate El Dorado and having to explore further inland) eventually turned to profit (a personal profit for him and a profit for the Spanish Crown), while in the case of Tzekel-Kan, his punishment turned into centuries of enslavement and outright decimation for the indigenous people of the Americas and Africa. Adults who know the history, along with children learning about the conquest, will be able to fill in the blanks as *The Road to El Dorado* comes to an end and our heroes (Miguel and Tulio) try to make their way back to Spain with Chel.

The character of Chief Tannabok lends itself to a different kind of analysis, for like Tulio and Miguel, he is also kind and generous. In his case, however, his kindness was almost extreme and his generosity was almost naïve. Thus, both qualities in the body of the chief are liabilities, for they almost made him lose his culture, his people, and his way of life. He trusted Tulio and Miguel, who were intent on conning him and stealing the impressive amounts of gold his people had amassed for generations. Of course, as Tulio's and Miguel's characters evolve and begin to care for the people of El Dorado, we see the chief was right in believing in and trusting these two men after all. But in the end, his sense of justice, charisma, and leadership were not enough; the chief needed Tulio and Miguel's kindness and generosity to save him, his people, and his kingdom/culture. As Cortez approaches, Tulio and Miguel work together to keep El Dorado hidden and out of reach for everyone, themselves included. As we have grown to like them and root for them throughout the story, we sense that it is them, and not the natives, who make the biggest sacrifice, as they give up the gold—the maximum measure of status during the conquest.

Finally, Chel's character is the most stereotypically conceived of the characters of color in this film: she is "hot" (as most Latinas are portrayed in U.S. popular culture); she is conniving (reminiscent of the stereotype of the harlot discussed by Charles Ramirez Berg (2002) in his book *Latino Images in Film*); she comes between Tulio and Miguel's friendship (as popular culture tells us women—especially flirtatious, hot-tempered Latinas—do); and, in the end, she still needs a valiant man to save her from herself (for Chel is about to be caught after stealing a piece of pottery when we first encounter her, and it is up to Tulio and Miguel to save her from being punished). Tulio and Miguel also save Chel from her own community (we learn early in the story that Chel is bored in El Dorado and wants to leave the place). As the story progresses, we also learn that Chel is smart (almost bordering on brilliant), and it is because of her help that Tulio and Miguel are able to convincingly pass themselves off as gods. Brilliance notwithstanding, it becomes apparent that Chel needs Tulio and Miguel to teach her how to channel her energies in the right direction.

As it does with whiteness, *El Dorado* packages brownness in a collage. When analyzing the three main "brown" characters, Chel, Tannabok, and Tzekel-Kan, we realize that together they embody contemporary American views about "Latinos": mainly that they are sneaky, naïve, childlike, distracting, untrustworthy, and deceiving. Of course, the characters in *The Road to El Dorado* are not "Latino" per se, as they are supposed to be indigenous peoples in Mexico, but insofar as they are portrayed with the characteristics that our society associates with Latinos, they become Latinos in the eyes of those watching the animated film. The discussion of *The Emperor's New Groove* shall serve as another illustration of this association.

THE EMPEROR'S NEW GROOVE: CONTEMPORARY WHITENESS AS A FOREFATHER OF LATINOS

With *The Emperor's New Groove*, Disney presents the story of Kuzco, a rich, spoiled, seventeen-year-old emperor. The audience is offered enough clues to assume that *New Groove* is a story about the Incas (or a civilization that approximates it) pre-conquest. Our first indication of this occurs even prior to watching the film, since in Disney's description of the story, we learn that it develops "long ago, somewhere deep in the jungle." We also receive clues to suggest that, on some level, the story has to do with Latinos today. The opening song offers the first clue, for even though it tells us that the events unfolding in the film are part of "meso-America history," the song itself is a Disneyfied salsa song. This juxtaposition of historical half-truths (invoking Mesoamerica) with contemporary tropes (that is, salsa music) is a persistent theme in the film. The recurrent theme of llamas, the "brownness" and particular attire of the characters, and the hilly landscape allow the audience to easily place *New Groove* in a pre-conquest, Andean setting, even though the name of the place or the time are never revealed in the story. The emperor's name is also a clue, for Cuzco (with a "C") is a city in Perú.

As with most Disney stories, *New Groove* has unconditionally evil characters, unconditionally good characters, and redeemable-with-some-work characters. Kuzco, though selfish, self-centered, and with an unhealthy dose of self-importance, is, as the main character of the story, a redeemable-with-some-work character.

After all, according to Disney, *New Groove* is a story about "discovering the good in everyone." His redemption is induced and catalyzed by Pacha, a peasant who saves his life and teaches the emperor a lesson about giving without expecting anything in return, and about caring for others, even those who have wronged us. Pacha, who lives a simple, but happy life with his wife and his soon-to-be three children (they have two children already and one is on its way), is an unconditionally good character. Izma, Kuzco's advisor, is an unconditionally bad character. Kronk, Izma's aide, is a childlike innocent character.

The film's narrative begins the day before Kuzco's eighteenth birthday, when he is describing to the audience his power as emperor. In his words, "in this palace, everyone is at my command." He also says at some point, "I am king of the world." It is when Kuzco is reveling in this self-aggrandizing exercise that Pacha enters the palace. As we learn, he has been summoned by the emperor. Kuzco welcomes Pacha and tells him he needs his help, asking Pacha details about the hill where he (Pacha) lives. Pacha tells him about the hill and about the fact that people have lived there for more than six generations. We (and Pacha) find out that Kuzco just needed Pacha's input in order to decide where he was going to place the pool to the resortlike development he is planning to build on Pacha's hill, which he calls "Kuzcotopia." Pacha then tries to appeal to his good sense by pointing out, once again, that many families who live on that hill would be displaced and landless if such development were to take place. Kuzco ends the conversation by stating, "Your town will be destroyed to make way for this," as he points to a scaled model of his planned development. Pacha's anguish is apparent.

The rest of the story develops after Kuzco fires Izma, his advisor, and Kronk, her aide, turns the emperor into a llama by mistake (he was actually supposed to poison—that is, kill—the emperor). In the process of trying to return to the palace and his human form, Kuzco, the emperor, learns a few lessons from Pacha, the peasant. Though a straightforward Disney story in this respect, *New Groove* also provides viewers with an orchestrated imagery of end-of-the-twentieth-century U.S. whiteness and Latinoness. This imagery takes two specific forms: (1) Latino culture as white American culture, and (2) ancient civilizations of Mesoamerica as precursors to whiteness. Although both sets of imageries are somewhat subtle, they are still very much present in the film.

The images portraying Latino culture as white American culture are, undoubtedly, doubly problematic, for they suggest that Latino culture is mainstream-able and consumable. For instance, while simultaneously claiming that *New Groove* is about (an ancient) culture in Mesoamerica, the film intermittently—but systematically—reveals elements of "Latino culture" recognized by U.S. mainstream culture. The opening song mentioned above serves as the first illustration for this argument. As noted, the song is a happy song, with salsa rhythm—a rhythm mostly associated with Puerto Ricans in New York City, and which began to spread in the 1960s. We see Kuzco happily dancing to the song as if the rhythm came naturally to members of pre-Columbian, Mesoamerican civilizations. In a later scene in the film, a mix-up at a restaurant occurs (yes, apparently, there were restaurants in the pre-Columbian Andes), and the staff sings a birthday song to Izma while they put a Mexican sombrero on her head (something that Mexican restaurants do for Americans in the United States). Later, in an action scene, Izma ends up serving as a living piñata to a group of children (again, another image associated with Latinos—Mexicans, to be precise). Though silly and even funny, these images teach and reinforce in children ideas about Latinoness in the United States. Even more important, insofar as certain aspects of Latino culture are being mainstreamed in the United States (as discussed at the beginning of the chapter), they are also being established as part of white culture (in this case, mainstreaming equals whitening).

Thus, it seems as though *The Emperor's New Groove* presents ancient civilizations in the Americas as precursors to U.S. whiteness and white culture. Specifically, the story about this purported ancient civilization is told with a highly updated perspective, especially a perspective that associates Western culture with capitalist economies (another marker for whiteness). First, the empire in *New Groove* is run like a corporation. For instance, when Kuzco fires Izma, she says she does not understand what he means, and he proceeds to explain it using a series of synonyms associated with the corporate world today: "you are being let go," "you are done with your functions," and "your services are no longer needed." In addition, as she is being fired, another one of the emperor's personal aides gives Izma a "pink slip." The corporatization of this pre-Columbian empire in the film is compounded by other references to capitalism, such as when Pacha returns home after his exchange with the emperor. He cannot find the courage to tell his wife about the emperor's plans, so he says that the emperor was busy and unable to see him. Pacha's wife then relays that, emperor or not, he should have had the "common courtesy" to see Pacha. It is as if Pacha had returned from trying to see the corporation's CEO, who did not have the "common courtesy" to see him. We find the most compelling example of the pre-Columbian empire as the corporate empire, however, in Kuzco's intention to build his Kuzcotopia to benefit himself (and the empire) at the expense of the people—one of the most devastating aspects of capitalism.

Within this context, capitalism is de-historicized and viewers are inculcated into a notion that makes the "natives" seem like predecessors of U.S. whiteness. It is Disney's way of saying, see, these people really didn't lose (haven't lost) much in the last five hundred years. Capitalism was there; thus whiteness was there. The conquest was just a way of accelerating the inevitable spread of both. Whiteness is also present in other images as well. One indication of whiteness we find in the film is Kuzco's speech pattern, along with his selfish and self-indulgent personality. In the case of his speech pattern, Kuzco talks like any "typical" white teenager in the United States, sans bad language. His personality, though slightly modified at the end, can be seen as a result of Kuzco's individualism—a highly praised value in contemporary U.S. narratives and ideologies (which historians and anthropologists tell us was not a valued quality among indigenous populations living in the pre-Columbian Americas). Even after we learn that Kuzco "changes" his selfish ways, he does not abandon completely his individualistic manner. For instance, even though he does not wipe out Pacha's village to build his resort, Kuzco does build a less ostentatious resort (more like a nice cabana) on the next hill. And even though he shares his pool with the villagers and seems to develop a great friendship with Pacha and his family, his cabana-resort is more extravagant than the dwellings of Pacha and the other peasants, reinscribing his position as emperor and as an individual among the people.

DREAMWORK'S *EL DORADO* AND DISNEY'S *NEW GROOVE*: IMPLICATIONS FOR LATINOS IN THE UNITED STATES

The narratives and plots derived from both of these films tell the audience that the indigenous peoples of the Americas have undergone no cultural changes resulting from the conquest and colonization they have endured for over five hundred years. According to these films, these indigenous peoples are the Latinos we see today in the United States, and they have always behaved in the ways we can easily identify: the women have always been hot and eager to be rescued from their own cultures, men and women have always been festive, and they have always behaved as children in need of instruction/protection. More importantly, the fact that these peoples (who we see as one people) behave as they always have (including how they behave today) means that Western society has really not altered them (or their cultures) in any substantive way. In fact, it follows that indigenous folks as a whole were the antecedent of our society. They knew about bureaucracies, about hierarchies, about living in a capitalist society, and about the replaceability of individuals. Consequently, in two 1.5-hour films, history is rewritten and recast in ways that make brutal processes such as genocide and stealing of lands palatable to children and adults alike, making everyone comfortable. In the end, these films teach us that the people of El Dorado are safely tucked away somewhere we cannot find, and the decimated civilizations of Mesoamerica are not all that decimated after all, for our teenagers are just as self-indulgent as their teenagers were over five hundred years ago. We can conclude that these representations, along with the anthropomorphized "Latino penguins" and other Latino representations in animated films, reinforce accepted understandings of certain racial and ethnic categories along with accepted narratives involving their position in society and history and their role(s) in relation to mainstream culture.

6

BEYOND SNOW WHITE

Femininity and Constructions of Citizenship

In 1959, Disney released *Sleeping Beauty*, the story of Aurora, a princess who, after being cursed by a jealous witch, Maleficent, is raised in anonymity by her fairy godmothers (Flora, Fauna, and Merryweather). Maleficent's curse stipulates that on her sixteenth birthday, Aurora will prick her finger on a poisoned spinning wheel and die. Although the fairy godmothers cannot undo the curse, Merryweather is able to modify it, stipulating that instead of dying, Aurora will fall into a deep, ageless sleep, from which she can be awakened by the kiss of her true love. Taking every precaution possible, the King orders all spinning wheels in the kingdom to be burned and sends Aurora to be raised by her fairy godmothers in a cottage deep in the forest, under the name Briar Rose. The princess remains in the forest until her sixteenth birthday, when the godmothers reveal to her who she is and decide to take her back to the castle to occupy her position as princess. She of course pricks her finger on a spinning wheel that Maleficent built just for her, falls asleep, and is awakened by the kiss of her one and true love, a prince she had met earlier on the day of her birthday, and to whom, it turns out, she was betrothed.

Almost fifty years later, in 1998, DreamWorks released its popularly acclaimed animated film *Antz*. The film tells the story of Z, a common worker ant, who, we immediately learn, thinks he was not made to be a worker, has feelings of inadequacy, and tells his therapist the system makes him "feel insignificant." In spite of all that, he also falls in love with Bala, the colony's princess. Relevant to this discussion is that even though he is highly insecure, feels insignificant, and is a worker among billions, and even though Bala is self-assured and intelligent and at some point tells Z, "Don't you realize I'm out of your league?" Z ends up heroically rescuing her, her mother (the queen), and the entire colony from a dooming plot by General Mandible. He also, of course, gets the princess in the process, who falls in love with him because he is "different."

As mentioned in our introduction, since Disney began to release classic animated films such as *Snow White and the Seven Dwarfs* (1937), *Cinderella* (1950), and *Sleeping Beauty* (1959), femininity in animated films has been cast as white. (Within this context, Snow White's name is interesting in itself.) The portrayal of female characters has followed a very similar pattern; that is, they have been depicted as princesses in need of rescue from unfair circumstances by Prince Charming. They have also been represented as good girls endowed with an inordinate amount of kindness and an even greater dose of passivity (Lacroix 2004). Within these classic films, the girls can only wait for rescue, and they do so patiently and gracefully. The girls have no other options, and their agency is limited by their gender. As Giroux (1999, 98) remarks, "the female characters [in animated

films were] constructed within narrowly defined gender roles."
Thus, in these early animated representations, femininity is typically flat and one-dimensional.

Recent animated films, however, seem to portray more nuanced femininities (and gender roles generally) than those earlier
films. The femininity portrayed in more recent films offers more
agency: in a post-women's-movement era, the femininity por
trayed by animated characters is, indeed, more assertive. It is also
more sexualized. According to Celeste Lacroix (2004, 214), beginning with *The Little Mermaid* in 1989, there has been "an increasing emphasis on sexuality and the exotic [which] is evident in the
construction of the female heroines in [animated] films." Regardless of the differing levels of agency, sexuality, and assertiveness
granted to the female characters throughout the decades, one aspect of their femininity has remained consistent: its racialization.
In early (Disney) films, characters were unquestioningly racialized as white. In more recent films, however, the racialization of
these characters has taken other forms. The sexualized and racialized images in contemporary animated films, and the meaning
derived from them, Lacroix (2004, 215) argues, intersect with "the
larger socio-historical framework regarding women of color and
the notion of Whiteness." Thus, when watching and analyzing
these films, we need to keep in mind (1) that the racialization of
female characters in animated films is an extension of social, historical, and cultural contexts, and (2) for "characters of color" the
process needs to be understood in relation to the racialization of
"white characters." Moreover, as discussed earlier in the book,
these processes also occur in films with non-human characters,
for non-human characters are not only "turned into" male and female humans (that is, anthropomorphized) but turned into white
and non-white humans (that is, they are racialized) as well. Even
non-human characters (for example, animals, aliens, and toys)
display a "humanity" to which the audience can relate, and they

articulate and perform gender and race in ways that are familiar to us.

A compounding element we find in contemporary animated films is the articulation of a (U.S. white) citizenship embedded within constructions of femininity. This particular construction of femininity by way of citizenship will be a central theme in this chapter. As we mentioned in the preceding chapter, these ideological constructions are important because they instruct children about normalcy and morality. Furthermore, and perhaps more importantly, the ideologies embedded within the films help children to develop ideas about themselves as citizens (not necessarily citizens in the legal sense, but as cultural citizens—those who belong in the United States). As Lacroix (2004, 217) indicates, they also help children develop "discourses regarding other [or non-citizens]."

Lessons about a citizenship of belonging are provided by way of particular signifiers. One of those signifiers, clothing, seems superficial, but it provides viewers a level of comfort and a means of recognition that allows them to absorb more profound messages in the films. Attire gives us an idea about time period, place, and the characters' social standing, among other things. In fact, attire in contemporary animated films can be seen as a signifier of particular femininities and citizenships (much like language, mannerisms, and other signifiers). It offers an idea of how "hip" the characters are, with hipness also being a measure of both femininity and citizenship. Take, for instance, Giroux's (1999, 96) comment that "Disney's representations of evil women and good women appear to have been fashioned in the editorial office of *Vogue*." The representation of female characters as fashionably chic, thus, places notions of good and evil at the heart of commodification and market forces by way of the fashion industry. In addition, the citizenship of female characters (of both the heroines and the villains) in animated films is represented and measured in relation to, and juxtaposed against the foreign (and ex-oticized) constructions of femininity that Lacroix (2004) mentions in her essay. At the same time, we argue that we can find a pattern in which the exoticized and sexualized heroine characters are conferred "honorary citizenship" (that is, honorary "U.S." citizenship).

This chapter explores the connections between constructions of (white) citizenship and articulations of femininity in Disney's *Mulan* (1998) and *Lilo and Stitch* (2002), and DreamWorks' *Shrek* (2001) and *Chicken Run* (2000). Mainly, we argue that (1) although articulated in different ways, the films present familiar configurations of citizenship mediated by way of feminine traits, and (2) such configurations are mediated by race (or more specifically, by the racial construction of the characters).

OF ORPHANS AND WARRIORS: LILO AND MULAN AS LOVABLE GIRLS

As a story, Disney's *Lilo and Stitch* presents the audience with a nontraditional tale of family structure and even less traditional ideas of what constitutes a family. While Disney had been notorious for portraying motherless children (Snow White, Cinderella, Ariel from *The Little Mermaid*, and Princess Jasmine are just a few examples), Lilo's situation is different, for both of her parents died in a car crash and she is under the care of her older sister, Nani. Nani is fighting Child Protective Services (a mundane signifier adding to the plot of the film) to keep Lilo in her care. In fact, this is the first (and only) animated story in which we see the government interfering with the family structure. Throughout the film, Lilo tries to apply the concept of family learned from her late father (that is, "Ohana: nobody is left behind or forgotten"), which she uses to come to terms with her reality. In an effort to (re)build her family in her own way, Lilo adopts as her pet an alien creature programmed to destroy everything he touches (whom she names Stitch). In an effort to escape imprisonment on his planet, the alien is trying to pass himself off as a dog, and Lilo tries to teach him about family. According to Disney, however, the story is not about family, but about "wild and irresistible characters," as well as "friendship and finding your place."

The story begins on another planet, where scientist Dr. Jumba is being sentenced to prison for conducting illegal genetic experiments, from which Experiment 626 (Stitch) is created. Experiment 626, then, is condemned to exile. While being transported, he manages to break free and heads to Earth. This is when we see Lilo for the first time, as she is swimming in the ocean, feeding a peanut butter sandwich to the fish. The image of Lilo swimming expertly in the ocean is juxtaposed to the sound of typical Hawaiian music playing in the background. Next, we see dancers practicing what seems to be an autochthonous Hawaiian dance. As the story begins to unfold, we learn that Lilo is an angry, lonely girl who listens to Elvis Presley records to drown her suffering. She seems to miss her family tremendously, including her sister, Nani, in her role as sister. As Lilo tells Nani after a big fight: "I liked you better when you were my sister." Lilo's anguish is such that we witness her becoming violent a few times. At the beginning of the film, for instance, she attacks one of her "friends" from her dance class (the "friend" calls her weird and Lilo jumps on her, biting her and pulling her hair). We learn that Lilo is also bright and loving, and, as Disney would lead us to believe, only needs a stable family environment in which to thrive. We realize how much Lilo is hurting when she asks her sister, Nani: "We are a broken family, aren't we?" As the film unfolds, we see Nani making Herculean efforts to keep custody of Lilo by trying to find a job, and trying to care for Lilo and the destructive Stitch.

There is no doubt that as a Disney product, *Lilo and Stitch* presents viewers with a groundbreaking narrative in the genre of animated films for children: two sisters trying to keep what is left of their family together against difficult odds. Added to this is the fact that the entire cast is comprised of either humans "of color" or alien forms. In fact, we only see a small number of "white" folks in the background (mostly tourists) in a few scenes, and none of them talk. The only white character who speaks in a few scenes is Margaret, Lilo's "friend" (the one she attacked), who is mostly portrayed as a heartless little girl.

Though Lilo is portrayed as a quirky but lovable little girl, there is one particular behavior that tells us a great deal about the film: Lilo collects pictures of white tourists. In fact, in the very first scene, after she comes out of the water, she grabs her camera and snaps a picture of an overweight white tourist eating an ice cream cone. Lilo has her collection of pictures up on the wall by her bed, and as she is sitting on her bed conversing with her sister, Nani, one night, she (Lilo) asks: "Aren't they beautiful?" This reversal of the process of othering is significant, for in it, we witness the commodification of whiteness.

Mulan presents a different perspective on girls of color. As another Disney product(ion), *Mulan* narrates the tale of a Chinese girl who decides to join her country's military to save her father. According to Disney, the film "transforms an ancient Chinese legend into unparalleled fun and adventure that comes along but once every dynasty." About Mulan, the character, Disney tells us that she is a "lovable, spirit nature girl who doesn't quite fit into her tradition-bound society." The company goes on to convey that "[o]nly by staying true to herself will she bring victory to her country and honor to her family." At the beginning of the film, Mulan's family (in an almost unprecedented depiction by Disney, Mulan is shown to have a mother and a father, as well as a grandmother) is attempting to maintain family honor by turning Mulan into a marry-able girl. Mulan tries her best to fit this role, but she fails. Although the viewers learn that the story is not about Mulan's role as a bride, but about her role as a brave warrior (as we discuss below), these two aspects of the girl are intertwined together from the start of the story.

For instance, the story begins with the Hun's invasion of China (led by Shan-Yu). Once the viewers understand that war is imminent, we see Mulan, for the first time, reciting out loud the virtues of a good bride: "quiet, demure, graceful, polite, refined, poised, and punctual." We learn quickly that, though kind, brave, and self-sacrificing, Mulan does not quite possess any of the virtues she is asked to memorize. In fact, after a series of unfortunate events in which Mulan sets the town's matchmaker on fire, the matchmaker tells her: "You may look like a bride, but you will never bring your family honor." The viewers understand at this point that a woman brings honor to her family by being able to get married, while we also learn in a subsequent scene that men bring honor to their families by participating in war and defending their country. These roles, we are able to understand, are mutually exclusive and not interchangeable.

Since she was chastised in front of the entire town (and obviously has nothing to lose), Mulan breaks tradition and joins the Chinese army, with the idea of saving her injured father from going to battle once again. Thus, cutting off her hair and dressed as a man, Mulan rides her horse to be trained for battle. She also receives the "help" of Mushu, a demoted dragon sent (by mistake) by her family's ancestors. As a side note, we would like to point out that following the tradition of racialized anthropomorphism we discussed in chapter 1, Mushu (voiced by Eddie Murphy) speaks with a cadence and vocabulary that U.S. mainstream society associates with twenty-first-century African Americans.

Mulan is able to pass for a man, of course, and goes on to join the military's offensive against the Hun after a long and excruciating training. We see Mulan in battle, where she almost singlehandedly saves her comrades (including her captain, with whom she has fallen in love), the country, and the emperor from the invaders. However, before she gains her glory, she is injured in the midst of a fight with the Hun, and her condition as a female is discovered. Since she had saved the life of her captain prior to this, he spares her life in return (we had been told before that if she were discovered, she would be killed) but discharges her dishonorably. Her unit and captain leave behind Mulan, where she is able to reflect on the situation. There she has the following exchange with Mushu:

> Mulan: I should never have left home.
>
> Mushu: Hey, come on. You went to save your father's life. Who knew you'd end up shamin' him and disgracing your ancestors and losing all your friends. You know, you just gotta—you just gotta learn to let things go.
>
> Mulan: Maybe I didn't go for my father. Maybe what I really wanted was to prove I could do things right, so when I looked in the mirror I'd see someone worthwhile. But I was wrong. I see nothing.

After this moment of contemplation, Mulan learns that Shan-Yu (who was leading the Hun offensive) is still alive, and thus, the country is still in danger. She rushes to the Imperial City to alert her comrades and here is where she proves herself, managing to save the emperor, the city, and the country by fighting and destroying the Hun and Shan-Yu. At the end, the emperor recognizes her bravery (in spite of the fact that she is female) and awards her the Imperial Medal along with Shan-Yu's spade. These awards are signs of honor and recognition. Thus, Mulan comes back home with the family honor intact. Though Mulan's return home would have been a poignant and touching ending, the Disney ending requires the girl to be saved by a guy. In the final scene, the captain (the one who had spared her life after finding out she was a woman) arrives at Mulan's house seeking her. She invites him in for dinner.

MULAN AND LILO'S CITIZENSHIP: THE WHITENESS OF GIRLS OF COLOR

Although set in "foreign" lands (in this context, Hawaii seems as foreign as China), Lilo and Mulan are given an honorary U.S. citizenship. We should, of course, assume that as a Hawaiian Lilo *is* a U.S. citizen, but we should also keep in mind that, as a girl of color in a highly exoticized land, Lilo may not be seen by the viewers as a U.S. citizen—in her case, citizenship is nonexistent unless bestowed upon her by the viewers. We argue that in both of these cases (Lilo's and Mulan's), citizenship is recognized by way of a superimposed whiteness. More specifically, Lilo and Mulan are recognized as citizens because they are given agency to pursue the kind of individualism that makes these two girls honorary whites.

In the case of Mulan, the white individualism and citizenship granted her is also gendered, for in the end, after single-handedly saving China, she is able to gain a husband. As Giroux (1999, 102) states, Mulan is portrayed "as a bold warrior who challenges traditional stereotypes of women" but "the ultimate payoff for her bravery comes in the form of catching the handsome son of a general." Hence, her real victory was not in becoming a strong individual, winning the war and liberating China from the Hun invasion, and becoming a patriotic hero; rather, it is in winning a prospective husband—the endeavor to which she was dedicated at the beginning of the film.

Lilo's case is somewhat different, for she is still a child—one who has lost her parents. Though portrayed as a strong little girl, her strength can be easily mistaken for stubbornness, and her mental independence, for bratty behavior. As Mulan did, Lilo also triumphed at the end. In her case, she found family when her sister, Nani, married her boyfriend, David. As the film ends, we see the pictures in which Lilo looks happy and thrilled with her new, nuclear family. It is in her finding that staple of the individualistic U.S. society (the nuclear family) that Lilo becomes a (white) normal citizen.

BEYOND SNOW WHITE: FEMININITY AND CONSTRUCTIONS OF (WHITE-WHITE) CITIZENSHIP

Lilo and Mulan notwithstanding, animated films are still predominantly comprised of white female main characters and heroines. It is our contention that citizenship is bestowed upon white characters differently from the way it is bestowed upon characters of color. In the case of white female characters, individualism is taken for granted. White female characters do not have to "perform" individualism in order to gain acceptance in (or access into) mainstream culture. In this case, their whiteness is synonymous with individualism, but this does not mean they are full citizens. Female white characters, we argue, gain citizenship by way of performing roles that combine their gender with their whiteness. In order to develop these arguments, we will use Dream-Works' *Shrek* (2001) and *Chicken Run* (2000). More specifically, we will use the characters of Princess Fiona and Ginger respectively, even though we are aware that neither one of them is uncomplicatedly white.

Although DreamWorks describes Princess Fiona as "feisty," watching the story we find that even feisty princesses need to be rescued by gallant men. *Shrek* is presented to us simultaneously as both a fairy tale (in fact, DreamWorks proclaims *Shrek* to be "the greatest fairy tale never told!") and a satire of fairy tales (*Shrek* moves through the clichéd world of a princess being held captive and awaiting rescue). However, we would be misrepresenting the story if we were to describe it as a story of a rescued princess a la Sleeping Beauty or Snow White, for the story is much more nuanced than its non-satirical predecessors. In this case, the princess was jinxed, and ever since she can remember, she has turned into an ogre at night (although nobody knows this). Lord Farquaad blackmails Shrek, the main character, into rescuing the princess. Lord Farquaad wants to become king of his town (Duloc), but is told—by the mirror used by Snow White's stepmother—that he needs a princess to be able to become king. The mirror, then, offers him a selection of princesses from which to choose: Snow White, Cinderella, and Fiona (who is trapped in a castle guarded by a dragon). Farquaad chooses Fiona, but does not want to rescue her himself. Shrek, who wants his swamp back after Farquaad has exiled all the characters in every fairy tale there, agrees to rescue Princess Fiona in exchange for his swamp.

A talking donkey (named "Donkey" and described by Dream-Works as a "loveable loudmouthed donkey") enlists himself to help Shrek in his mission. The donkey in this case is similar to the dragon in Mulan, and is also played by Eddie Murphy. Shrek goes to the castle and rescues Princess Fiona (wearing a knight's armor), who then tries to fulfill the fairy tale by offering her lips. Shrek, still wearing the armor's helmet, doesn't follow her lead, asking her what she is doing. She replies that she is trying to reward him for his valiant effort, adding: "You must know how it goes: a princess locked in a tower and beset by a dragon is rescued by a brave knight [she points to Shrek] and then they share true love's first kiss." Donkey and Shrek roll around laughing about Fiona's expectations. Shrek finally tells Fiona, "I don't think I'm your type," to which Fiona responds, "Of course you are; you are my rescuer." Though presenting multiple twists, the "greatest fairy tale never told" becomes, in the end, another reincarnation of the princess in distress meeting her rescuer, who sooner or later (later rather than sooner in this case) sweeps her off her feet. The audience is supposed to see the story as transgressive, for in the end Fiona remains in her ogre state (not in her beautiful human, white body) after being kissed by Shrek. In this way, Fiona breaks with the tradition of "beautiful" princesses. As we learn earlier in the film, she thinks of herself as ugly every night as she is transformed into an ogre. The most important lesson *Shrek* teaches, however, is that in order for love to exist and for relationships to occur, both individuals need to be at the same level: in this case, a beautiful princess would fall in love with an ogre (even a kind ogre like Shrek) only if she is an ogre herself. Conversely, an ogre princess cannot expect a handsome prince to rescue her, fall in love with her, and live together happily ever after. And it is in her need to be rescued (more than her light skin and red hair) that we find her whiteness.

With *Chicken Run*, DreamWorks presents the audience with another excellent exercise of racialized anthropomorphism. In this case, we have the case of chickens trying to flee the coop of an English egg farm (Tweedy's Farm). Presenting the audience with images reminiscent of Jewish concentration camps in Nazi Germany, DreamWorks creates sympathetic characters stuck in an unfair predicament. Ginger, a hen, and one of the main characters, attempts to organize the chickens. With the help of Mac, another hen, she designs numerous strategies for escaping the coop. Each of their attempts fails, and Mr. Tweedy also catches Ginger and puts her in "solitary confinement." The farm has a location where the hens who are no longer useful (that is, have

stopped laying eggs) are taken and their necks are cut. Throughout their multiple attempts to flee the coop, Ginger keeps her
hopes up and fantasizes about life "on the other side of the
fence." She also tries to keep the other chickens convinced that
there is life beyond the fence. However, for the most part, the
chickens demonstrate a colonized mind, and are unable to envi-
sion life without a farm and a farmer. Here is an exchange between Ginger and some fellow hens:

> Ginger: You know what the problem is? The fences aren't just
> around the farm. They're up here, in your heads. There's a better
> place out there, somewhere beyond that hill, and it has wide open
> spaces, and lots of trees . . . and grass. Can you imagine that? Cool,
> green grass.
>
> Hen: Who feeds us?
>
> Ginger: We feed ourselves.
>
> Hen: Where's the farm?
>
> Ginger: There is no farm.
>
> Babs: Then where does the farmer live?
>
> Ginger: There is no farmer, Babs.
>
> Babs: Is he on holiday?
>
> Ginger: He isn't anywhere. Don't you get it? There's no morning
> head count, no farmer, no dogs and coops and keys, and no fences.
>
> Bunty: In all my life I've never heard such a fantastic . . . load of
> tripe! Oh, face the facts, ducks. The chances of us getting out of
> here are a million to one.
>
> Ginger: Then there's still a chance.

During their discussions about fleeing, Rocky, an American
rooster, plops in from the sky. After much prodding and some
blackmailing, Ginger convinces Rocky to teach them how to fly, so
they can escape. As with any such story, Rocky and Ginger fall in

love. At the end, as incapable and incompetent as they are, the hens manage to escape the coop, and they all choose a place in the wild where they are able to live happily ever after.

GINGER AND PRINCESS FIONA: THE WHITENESS OF WHITE GIRLS

The characters of Ginger and Fiona convey that whiteness (for white girls) is attained through a process of rescue. Their white womanhood is, thus, reinscribed every time they need a gallant (white male) to rescue them. In the process of having her whiteness bestowed upon her, Fiona transforms herself from a (white) princess who follows the social script to the letter, to a (white) woman who follows her heart. Paradoxically, her heart and the social script are one and the same. The fact that Fiona turns green in the process (for she actually becomes an ogre) is relevant here, since this tells us that Fiona's whiteness extends beyond her actual skin color and her human (or non-human) condition. The fact that Fiona looks like a female version of Shrek when she is green also informs us that Shrek himself is white. Consequently, the white woman *was* rescued by a white man. Underneath the green ogre is a white woman who learned how to be a white woman by following her heart, which in this case translates into following the script.

Similarly, Ginger's character changes from one craving liberty and independence to that of a regular wife (to Rocky) and mother (to their children). Her rescue and the bestowing of her whiteness is a little more complicated than in the case of Fiona, but it is still clear. Ginger is a hen (Rocky calls her a "chick" a few times) and Rocky is, of course, a rooster. Nonetheless, we are given plenty of clues as to their whiteness. In the case of Rocky, his accent, speech pattern, and the fact that he proudly claims to be from "a little place [he calls] the land of the free and the home of the brave" mark him as white. Our suspicions of Rocky are confirmed when Fowler calls him a "Yank." Ginger's whiteness is also signaled by speech patterns and mannerisms. In her case, we also have the complicated factor of her nationality and citizenship. As Rocky points out, she is a "British chick." Ginger, however, is able to transgress her "Britishness" when she falls in love with Rocky. In fact, up to that point, Ginger is pretty non-feminine and hangs out with a clearly androgynous "chick," Mac. Before Rocky comes into their lives, Ginger has no time to be feminine and no time for an alternative cultural citizenship. Falling in love with Rocky and escaping from her captivity contribute to her new cultural citizenship, as exchanging a kiss with Rocky grants her the femininity that was lacking before, and fleeing the coop and having Rocky's children grants her a symbolic American citizenship. Thus, Rocky liberates Ginger from both the coop and a life of unfeminine British citizenship. It is Rocky, the all-American rooster, who grants Ginger her "white Americanness."

CONCLUSION

Princess Aurora is awakened from her slumber by her prince, marries him, and lives happily ever after. Princess Bala finds a commoner who is able to sweep her off her feet and save her colony, and she marries him. Princess Fiona falls in love with her rescuer (an ogre) and marries him. And Ginger falls in love with her liberator, whom she marries. Although this overly tried rehearsal of the "femininity equals being rescued and marrying your rescuer" message is worth discussing, we think the messages involving a woman's place as a raced person and a woman's standing as a citizen are more important. While these female characters tell us quite a bit about elements of femininity that we may

value (i.e., heterosexuality or the valuing of heterosexual relationships), the stories around them tell us a bit more about a
woman's positioning in today's society, where femininity, whiteness, and U.S. citizenship are intertwined. Thus, whether they retain their status as princesses or independent women has no consequence unless we are (the audience is) assured that they are
bona fide "members" of our society and our world.

7

NEGOTIATING "DIFFERENCE"

The Racial Politics of Transgressive Sexualities/Families

The Disney/Pixar film *Cars* (2006) establishes a (literal) competition between old and new—the basis for the film's story line—in its opening scene. As the film begins, the audience witnesses an animated Nascar-type auto race, the Piston Cup, in which the announcers project the winner to be one of three cars, depicted as "the Legend," "the Runner Up," and "the Rookie." Lightning McQueen, "the Rookie" and the main character of the film, takes an unprecedented risk by avoiding a final pit stop and blows a tire a mere one hundred feet from the race's finish line. He struggles to cross the line in what emerges as a photo finish among the three favored racers. For the first time in Piston Cup history, race officials call a three-way tie, given their inability to discern a single winner. A tie-breaking race is set for a week later in California—a race aimed to establish a clear winner from among the three tied contenders.

The arrogance of "the Rookie," Lightning McQueen, is illustrated through his view that he can do without a pit crew or supporting team and his claim that he is "a one-man show." "The Legend" compliments Lightning McQueen on his considerable talent but remarks that he is also "very stupid" for believing that he can do without others. "The Legend's" loyalty to family, crew, and even his corporate sponsor, Dinoco, is juxtaposed to Lightning McQueen's thirst for an individualistic brand of fame and fortune, and the celebrity and promotion enabled by one's connection to "fancy" corporate sponsorship. Lightning McQueen does not hear what "the Legend" attempts to convey given his single-minded emphasis on speed—rehearsed in his refrain, "I am speed"—through which "speed" implies both literal pace (the fastest car wins the race) and a particular set of values (a "have it all now" mentality informing everything done).

The audience for *Cars* learns more about the tension between old and new, or between tradition and "life in the fast lane," when Lightning McQueen enters the sleepy town of Radiator Springs upon accidentally exiting the interstate on his way to California. Once vibrant, Radiator Springs, positioned on forgotten Route 66, was bypassed with the construction of Interstate 40. Its businesses have since struggled from a lack of travelers and customers. As Sally, the town's attorney, tells Lightning McQueen, "No one seems to need us anymore." She recounts a time "when cars crossed the country in a whole different way"—cars and road curved along together. The point was "not to make great time but to have a great time." With the construction and imposed linearity of Interstate 40, Radiator Springs was bypassed "to save 10 minutes of driving."

By film's end, Lightning McQueen has managed to internalize lessons offered by residents of Radiator Springs, and the film's audience has been presented with messages regarding the value of tradition or "the old"—including the importance of remembering those forgotten in the race for progress and the wisdom residing within unexpected or "different" packaging. While the lessons afforded by *Cars* can be considered progressive in the sense that they press beyond and counter a well-known set of U.S. mainstream values around matters of consumption, fame and fortune, obsession with celebrity, individualism, and a capitalist push to "rise to the top," the particular lessons in one arena of the film are only offered at the expense of certain racialized tropes, stereotypes, and simplifications within the film's narrative fold.

As a few examples of simplifications within *Cars*, we might cite the new/old binary itself, which transforms into a good/bad binary, offering nostalgia around all things Route 66 and the past more generally. Such nostalgia avoids complications around Route 66 and its classic role, among others, as a means of affording the white middle-class family vacation and tourist opportunities around attractions such as Indian curio shops and teepee-shaped hotels. Interestingly, while Lightning McQueen is clearly raced as white in *Cars*, as is Sally, who also becomes his love interest—thereby adding a love story and underscoring the normative heterosexuality discussed throughout this book—there are "other" cars in Radiator Springs that are clearly not white. As examples, we might mention Ramone, the Mexican car, who is recognizable as Mexican through his accent (he is voiced by Cheech Marin) and his jacked-up car with flaming lightning bolts down the side, and Flo, the black car, also identifiable through accent (she is voiced by Jenifer Lewis, who also lends her voice to Disney's upcoming *The Princess and the Frog*) and old purple Cadillac. While the very relationship between Ramone and Flo affords interesting possibilities—it might be heterosexual, but it is also interracial—its impact is softened through the use of stereotypical racial tropes bringing it together.

The primary claim in the present chapter is that several recent films for children offer opportunities, at least on the surface, for progressive lessons regarding "difference." More specifically, spaces for nontraditional expressions of sexuality and gender have been afforded within films such as *Ice Age* and *Shark Tale*, and opportunities to consider alternative family structures have been offered within *Dinosaur* and *Finding Nemo*. However, these otherwise "different" lessons come at the expense of rehearsals of more familiar understandings and are only offered within a context that maintains and holds steady certain problematic structures. The otherwise progressive lessons are thereby recuperated into a more mainstream fold, and this movement allows questions as to how progressive such lessons can be given their emergence within, and dependence upon, such stasis.

For instance, in *Shark Tale*, as noted in chapter 1, Lenny is uncomfortable with the viciousness expected of sharks and seems to convey to the audience that it is "okay to be oneself," even if this means resisting a preconceived "nature." In *Dinosaur*, Aladar is adopted by a clan of lemurs, which implies that a baby dinosaur (or anyone) can find "family" with those unlike oneself. However, despite the potential for meaningful lessons vis-à-vis issues of gender, sexuality, and family, these characters are only able to sustain themselves within a narrative frame that is highly racialized. That is, Lenny's "being himself" is inscribed within a racialized context that allows white, heterosexual, American audiences to remain comfortable with sexual or gender transgression because it is contained by and within a frame of ethnic and racial stereotypes. Likewise, Aladar's "alternative family" is situated within a narrative of implied manifest destiny in which the family makes its way to the nesting grounds after much of the Earth's population has been killed (in this case, by a meteor).

We argue that, rather than affording positive conceptions of alternative genders, sexualities, and families, it is more accurate to view these films as promoting the idea that progressive lessons in one arena (for example, gender, sexuality, and family) are only afforded via a negotiation—that comparable lessons not be offered in another arena (for example, race and ethnicity). Moreover, the end result for these characters (for example, Lenny and Aladar) is the same—Lenny is accepted back into the fold of the nuclear family, while Aladar begins his own (proper) dinosaur family. Thus, moments of "difference" themselves are, in the end, reinscribed within a more traditional framework.

We provide some context below for recent perceived difficulties around particular children's television characters and shows in the arena of gender and sexuality. We then connect this discussion to the consideration of two animated films: *Ice Age* and *Finding Nemo*. We offer cautionary remarks about the characters and moments discussed in these films, especially insofar as they might be read as progressive or transgressive. We initiate a discussion of broader protests around particular films that is then taken up more fully in the next chapter.

SEXUALITY AND NEGOTIATING "DIFFERENCE"

By way of further framing this chapter, it is important to note that there has been a great deal of recent focus in the United States on media representations of children's television show characters interpreted as gay or lesbian. One example of such attention involves the character of Tinky Winky, briefly addressed in chapter 1. Another more recent example is that of Sponge Bob Squarepants, dubbed by Christian-right (Focus on the Family) activist James Dobson as "pro-homosexual." Dobson has remarked that the purpose of characters such as Sponge Bob and others "is to desensitize very young children to homosexual and bisexual behavior" (Crary 2005, 2A). Similar remarks have been made in the case of the PBS children's program *Postcards from Buster*, in which the main character—an animated bunny (Buster)—visits the children of two lesbian couples in Vermont. While focused more on the television program itself than on a recurring character (or more specifically, highlighting a particular episode of the show), this installment of *Postcards from Buster* was deemed unacceptable in a number of PBS markets and obtained a statement of reproach from the U.S. Department of Education. In this circumstance, the main character, Buster, was not interpreted as gay or bisexual. Rather, the source of the difficulty, and the cited objectionable content, concerned the self-identified lesbian couples (also mothers) who would be featured (with their children) in the episode.

The situation involving *Postcards from Buster* highlights several issues of central concern in the present project. One issue involves the statement by Dobson that certain television show characters work to desensitize children to homosexual/bisexual behavior. While it is not obvious that desensitization is the "purpose" of these characters, as Dobson claims, he is nonetheless correct—in a sense—that shows for children can certainly have an impact on the children watching. In fact, to claim that children's animated feature films serve as agents of socialization, as maintained throughout the present work, is precisely to point to such an impact. The difference in view between Dobson (and others holding his position) and ourselves, then, involves where the concern rests. On the one hand, while we are distressed by the heterosexism, homophobia, sexism, and racism informing the portrayals of many animated characters and scenes (that is, the fact that children are given problematic *mainstream* messages regarding sexuality, gender, and race), Dobson, on the other hand, is alarmed by the counter-message afforded by some characters and scenes (that is, the fact that certain characters precisely *do not* depict mainstream messages and are out of line with "mainstream values"). From our perspective, Dobson's reading strategies reinforce a reactionary logic grounded in dehumanization and exclusion and reflect a preoccupation with a variety of questionable fears, whereas our efforts are directed at social justice and the transformation of particular perceptions around various marginalized groups. A second relevant issue surrounds the fact that the U.S. Department of Education effectively sided with the position that lesbian mothers and their children do not represent mainstream (read: Christian-right) interests and are not appropriate "subject matter" for children's television programming. In a statement from Secretary of Education Margaret Spellings, the episode of *Postcards from Buster* in question, titled "Sugartime!" "would undermine the overall objective of the Ready-to-Learn program—to produce programming that reaches as many children as possible" (de Moraes 2005). In this sense, the U.S. government interjected itself into the matter of PBS programming, signifying a comingling of state and church concerns. This interrelationship is also reflected in recent negative expressions of public opinion toward same-sex couples (specifically, the prospect of same-sex marriages) as evidenced by the constitutional ban on same-sex marriages effected by voters in eleven states during the 2004 presidential election. Such assertions of public opinion, combined with events such as exit polls that cited "moral values" as a key concern for voters in the 2004 election, help to contextualize and rationalize the judgment of the U.S. Department of Education that certain public programming aimed at children should not be permitted. Ironically, the chief operating officer for PBS, Wayne Godwin, justified pulling the episode on similar grounds. By way of PBS spokesperson Lea Sloan, he conveyed that the topic of lesbian mothers and children was "sensitive in today's political climate," and "the presence of a couple headed by two mothers would not be an appropriate curricular purpose that PBS should provide" (fair.org 2005).

Related to the issue of what is deemed appropriate subject matter for children is the dismissal of subjectivity in the case of the lesbian mothers themselves. That is, the issue of sexuality, in this and other cases, is reduced to behavior—a behavior thought to be inappropriately modeled for young children. Dobson's remark regarding the purpose of certain characters to desensitize children to homosexual/bisexual behavior is one example of this reduction; another example involves the reduction of sexual identity to matters of "lifestyle," as in Spellings's remark that "many parents would not want their young children exposed to the lifestyles portrayed in this episode" (de Moraes 2005). Of course, if agency is granted at all, it can be seen in the fact that "homosexuality as behavior" is not the full account of this position, as the behavior itself is thought to reflect a certain choice—a wrong and sinful choice and a choice that could be made otherwise. The bad choice is likewise positioned within a civilization in danger of decline through the enactment of such problematic choices.

We might also point out that the very children involved in the *Postcards from Buster* episode are forgotten in this discussion, since judgments regarding appropriate subject matter for children neglect the children who live daily with these particular lesbian mothers and others who share mothers who identify as lesbian. The irony behind the decision of PBS to pull the "Sugartime!" episode of *Postcards from Buster* is seen in the mandate of public television, as set forth in the 1967 Carnegie Commission Report: "to provide a voice for groups in the community that may otherwise be unheard" (fair.org 2005).

Given these and other quite vocal concerns expressed in relation to children's *television* programming, and provided statements regarding the purported purpose of specific characters to promote a "pro-homosexual agenda," we can ask why children's animated *films* have received so little attention from within these same arenas (namely, from conservative groups, though we discuss this issue more fully in the next chapter). The most obvious response, here, involves the fact that (children's) television is a public medium in a way that film is not; that is, children's television is considered free and available to everyone (especially in the case of PBS), whereas film requires the purchase of a ticket. Interestingly, however, it is more likely the *relationship between* public and private that grounds opposition to particular animated images. That is to say, programming "enters the living room" through the purchase of a television set–thereby serving either to comfort the inhabitants of the home or to intrude upon them. An attitude of "not in my home" informs views regarding how children might be impacted by what they "see" in this perceived private space. In contesting certain images, there is a refusal to permit the messages that these programs are thought to offer. In the case of presumed or explicit gay/lesbian representations, this process resituates "homosexuality" as something private and to be practiced–if at all–behind (someone else's) closed doors. Moreover, in the case of PBS programming in particular, the expressed nature of the material is to be "educational." From the start, such programming is not conceptualized as "mere entertainment," which likely acts to underscore the perceived legitimacy of various concerns to those holding and expressing them.

While the issue of sexuality in recent animated films for children involves a constraining of what might otherwise be considered progressive lessons (as illustrated below), the "ethnicity" featured in these films, as Martín-Rodríguez (2003, 282) has pointed out, is limited to some of the characters and "does not extend to their producers and writers nor even to the films' intended audience." Martín-Rodríquez (2003, 282) refers to the intended audience as "an ethnically undefined 'multicultural' construct," while he simultaneously states that he prefers the term "*mall*ticulturalism" (to *multiculturalism*) for it "organizes cultural differences as an uncritical display for the consumption of the curious, much in the same way in which a mall arranges its retail space" (282). According to Martín-Rodríquez, "The films do not function so much as an overture to particular ethnic groups as they do a reinforcement of societal values about those very same groups" (282). He continues, "no matter how much ethnicity may have been emphasized in recent films, the 'ethnic' still remains an other in Hollywood's children's movies, the object of fascination and repulsion at the same time" (283).

With these remarks, Martín-Rodríquez indicates what Tina Chanter (2007) (forthcoming) has asked, in a different context and with somewhat different intentions, "What if sexual difference itself were constituted on the basis of a repressed discourse of racial difference?" (6–7). Chanter continues, "What if our very notions of male and female have come to be concepts only on the basis of a violent repression of racialized, classed and transgendered others? What, in other words, if the very terms in which sexual difference has become legible . . . [have come to be] by repressing other differences that are therefore not permitted to be salient" (6–7). One manifestation of this repression, though it does not represent the only way to interpret Chanter's claims, involves the way in which (non-animated) characters have been coded for difference one marker at a time. That is, it has been typical for a character to be gay but not "of color," or "of color" but not gay—as if too many markers of "difference" would confuse the audience and undermine the borders of the categories themselves. An interesting recent filmic example that counters this tradition is the character of the son, Everett (played by Dermot Mulroney), in *The Family Stone* (2005), who is white, gay, deaf, and involved in an interracial relationship with a black man. Overall, while more animated film characters are emerging as ethnically or racially other-than-white, these characters are nonetheless precisely positioned as "other" *to* white. And while there are more characters that straddle the boundaries of mainstream prescriptions for gender and sexuality, these characters are nonetheless re-incorporated into the fold of the traditional family structure by film's end. Moreover, these same characters are able to enjoy moments of "transgression" in recent animated films only through the repression of [genuine] ethnic and racial difference. Rather, what emerges are stereotypical representations and the commodification of the racial/ethnic "other." Thus, so-called transgression in the areas of sexuality and gender operates on the basis of marginalized or repressed others. At the same time, this so-called transgression is recuperated into the fold of mainstream ideals by the end of these films.

ICE AGE AND FINDING NEMO: "ALTERNATIVE" FAMILIES, SEXUALITIES, GENDERS, AND THE NEGOTIATED "OTHER"

Ice Age

Ice Age clearly arises as a film that addresses the notion of "alternative" family structures. Much like *Dinosaur*, discussed earlier, *Ice Age* involves the incorporation of a member of a "different" species into the fold of a group that comes to care for him/her. In the case of *Dinosaur*, a clan of lemurs adopts the baby dinosaur, Aladar. However, in the end, Aladar is finally able to meet other dinosaurs, "settle down," and form his "own" family. While Aladar has been cared for by those unlike himself, his aim in the film becomes to find others like himself with whom he can reunite and procreate. That his reconnection with his species occurs at the "nesting grounds," after a long manifest-destiny-like trip, also acts to layer the heterosexual, nuclear family on top of racialized omissions and exclusions. Or, insofar as Aladar is expected to reunite with others of *like* species, heterosexuality itself is founded on conceptions of racial and ethnic (or species) purity.

Within *Ice Age*, a human baby is the member of a different species who becomes separated from his family when he loses his mother to a pack of saber-toothed tigers. Sid, the sloth, meets Manford (Manny), the mammoth, when Sid seeks Manny's protection from two rhinos that have threatened him. This circumstance establishes a number of important elements in the film, which will be addressed here and below. For now, it is important to note that Sid and Manny rescue a human baby from his mother's dying arms and that this rescue occurs after we have learned more about Sid and Manny. We learn, for example, that Sid perceives his own family to have abandoned him. He tells Manny that his family migrated without him and that they did so in a "tricky manner"; that is, they slipped away so he would not notice. We are led to wonder whether Sid's annoying antics (demonstrated throughout the film) are the cause of his own family seeking some distance. Nonetheless, this information about family and abandonment is significant because later in the film, when Manny saves the life of Diego, a saber-toothed tiger, Diego asks why Manny was willing to risk his own life. Manny responds, "That's what you do in a herd; you look out for each other." With this statement, Manny conveys his views on family at the same time as he explicitly positions Diego as a member of his own family (his herd). This sentiment is reiterated near the end of the film, when Diego, in turn, saves Sid and Manny from a potential ambush. Explaining his willingness to undergo injury, Diego remarks, "That's what you do in a herd." Here, Diego returns the warm regard that Manny has expressed for him, underscoring a particular (expansive) conception of "family."

It is significant to note that, prior to their rescue of the human baby, Sid conveys the details of his family and their abandonment. Within this conversation, Sid asks Manny, "What about you? Do you have family?" In response to these questions, Manny is silent, leaving open the facts of his own family circumstance. However, in an exchange regarding relationships, Manny conveys to Sid, "If you find a mate in life, you should be loyal . . . grateful," to which Sid replies, "I think mating for life is stupid." In a sense, these early exchanges between Sid and Manny rotate between Sid's attempts to connect with Manny and Manny's attempts to distance himself from Sid. Thus, when Diego encounters the two shortly after their rescue of the baby, Diego comments, "That pink thing [the baby] is mine." Sid replies, "No, actually, that pink thing belongs to us." Diego retorts, "Us? You two are a bit of an odd couple." Manny shows his distancing attempt by adding, "There is *no* us," to which Diego remarks, "I see. You can't have one of your own, so you want to adopt." Consequently, Manny and Sid are both perceived as a couple—an *odd* (inter-species) couple—and as joined by a child they can only have through adoption (given the relationship's procreative flaws). In this sense, "oddity" is conceived both in terms of race/ethnicity (or species) and sexuality—Diego's reference to "can't have one of your own" clearly gesturing to the increase in adoptions among gay and lesbian couples.

We learn more about Manny's family later in the film as the three—Sid, Manny, and Diego—walk to return the baby to "its herd." On the way, they encounter drawings on the inside of a cave wall. One drawing depicts a large mammoth joined by a smaller mammoth and a much smaller one. Sid exclaims, "[The mammoth] has a family. Oh, and he's happy. Look, he's playing with his kid. See, Manny, that's your problem. That's what mammoths are supposed to do." Manny moves toward the wall, silent. We see through Manny's eyes, as he reflects on the wall, that he *did* have a family. We also learn what happened. The three family members were attacked by a group of human beings with spears. While Manny tried to protect his family, they were nonetheless killed. Thus, we learn that Manny's sadness does not come from longing for a family (in a future-directed way); rather, it results from his memory of the family he had (in the past).

To return to the beginning of *Ice Age* for a moment, it is worth noting that the opening scenes depict animals "migrating south" in an effort to avoid the impending ice age. Many of these animals are seen in pairs; however, the pairs do not represent heterosexual partnerships. Rather, many of the pairings are animals of the same sex. For instance, in one same-sex pairing, an unusual looking animal asks his partner, "How do we know it's an ice age?" to which his partner sarcastically responds, "Because of all the ice?!" To this (non)response, his partner declares, in a campy tone, "Well, things just got a little chillier." In addition, the two rhinos mentioned previously, Carl and Frank, become angry with Sid when he impulsively eats a dandelion that they have spotted. Frank exclaims to Carl, "Carl, he ruined our salad." This event leads to Sid seeking protection from Manny, as noted above, when Carl and Frank threaten Sid. Upon finding him huddled beside Manny, Frank comments, "We'll just take our furry piñata and go, if you don't mind."

While we have claimed in an earlier chapter that there is more to the racialization and ethnicization of characters than reference to the voices animating the characters, in the case of Sid, it seems no accident that his voice is provided by John Leguizamo. Although Leguizamo is Colombian-American, and not Mexican (which would more appropriately fit the piñata remark), the point remains that a Latino is being threatened with being treated as a piñata. Consequently, while the rhinos could make an interesting gay couple, this gayness only comes at the expense of a racial/ethnic slur. In addition to this connection, Sid's laziness is consistently referred to throughout the film (even by Sid himself). For instance, in the cave where Manny sees the mammoth with its family depicted on the wall, Sid draws a picture of a sloth—remarking that sloths are often left out of such representations. Regarding Sid's drawing, Manny comments that Sid should have drawn it with a bigger belly, and "why don't you make it realistic and make him lying down?" Of course, "sloth" by definition has both the meaning of "a slow-moving mammal" and "a dislike of work or any kind of physical exertion." But to attach the character of the sloth to the voice of John Leguizamo easily makes the "Latinos as lazy" connection quite explicit. Of himself, Sid states, "I'm too lazy to hold a grudge." And Diego, early in the film, comments on the fact that Sid is "low on the food chain."

Another interesting point is that while Sid and Manny are eventually joined—permanently—by Diego (as a herd), the fact that Sid and Manny are not a couple is made clear to the audience by a couple of references. Sid's heterosexuality is shorn up when we see him sitting in a mud bath with two female sloths, one who remarks that it is rare to find such a creature. As she states, "All the sensitive ones [usually] get eaten," while the other female sloth comments, "It's hard to find a family man." Of course, both of these comments are ironic given Sid's earlier comments about monogamy (as stupid) and his insensitive remarks throughout the film. Manny's heterosexuality is made clear in the cave scene, when he reflects on the family that he once had. Both scenes position the characters as straight, so while they may hang out as "two bachelors knocking about in the world," these bachelors should not be mistaken for a gay couple. Diego's addition to the pairing—making it a trio—also helps to move attention away from the two characters as possibly being a same-sex couple.

Finding Nemo

Finding Nemo opens with a heterosexual couple (of clown fish), who have just moved to a larger "house" (a sea anemone). Their large cluster of eggs hasn't yet hatched, and they are awaiting their babies' arrival in anticipation. Regarding the new house, Marlin (the husband and soon-to-be father) asks Coral (the wife and expecting mother), "Did your man deliver or *did he deliver?*"

to which Coral responds, "Oh, he delivered." These opening minutes of marital happiness in the film soon end when a large menacing fish approaches the anemone. The expected moves get made: Coral rushes in, in an attempt to save the eggs; Marlin swims in, in an effort to save Coral. Marlin is knocked out in his struggle with the fish. When Marlin comes to, he learns that Coral and the eggs are gone (and the audience can assume that they have been eaten). Only one egg remains, and it soon hatches into Marlin's only (remaining) son, Nemo. While the film could have unfolded without this setup (in fact, the credits only roll after this scene of heterosexual normalcy and challenge), the setup is important for several reasons: (1) it establishes a frame of heterosexual marriage into which Nemo is born and after which (through the death of Coral) Nemo's father proceeds to raise him independently, (2) it suggests a cause for Marlin's anxiety and over-protective behavior for much of the film, and (3) it explains the bond between Marlin and Nemo that motivates events in the story.

What we soon learn about Nemo is that he has a "lucky fin"—one fin smaller than "normal." This fin is only further cause for Marlin to be concerned for Nemo, since as Marlin tells him, "The ocean is not safe," and "You know you can't swim well." It is this *perception* of Nemo's deficiency, however, that is ultimately more harmful to Nemo than any actual (dis)ability. In an effort to "prove himself," Nemo swims towards a boat in the distance, only to be captured by a scuba diver. We soon learn that the diver is also a dentist who collects fish for his office aquarium. Most of the film represents Marlin's attempt to try to rescue Nemo. Interestingly, it is demonstrated early in the film that Marlin, the *clown* fish, is unable to tell a joke. In this sense, Marlin counters expectation. Even more strongly, we could say that Marlin appears slightly depressed. While many comics have turned depression and anxiety into comedy—some arguing that comedy precisely arises from tragedy—Marlin is unable to formulate one joke.

Additionally, at one point in the film, Marlin remarks, "I'm feeling happy, which is a big deal for me." Of course, this "happiness" is only the result of being temporarily mesmerized by a light emanating from a dangerous fish, so Marlin's good feelings quickly come to a dramatic end. The notion of "defying expectations" is significant for the story that unfolds, since Nemo will discover (or prove to himself and others) that the expectations that his father has had of him (that he is unable to swim well) are actually false.

Nemo first discovers that he can, in fact, exceed his father's expectations through the encouragement of Gil—a larger fish in the dentist's office aquarium where Nemo finds himself. Gil exhibits numerous scars from his foiled attempts to escape the tank. He coaches Nemo through a plan to clog the aquarium's filter in an effort to have the tank drained, affording the fish an opportunity to exit through an open window into the nearby ocean. If Marlin has underestimated Nemo's abilities, it is Gil who highlights and believes in them. Nemo can identify with Gil, in a sense, due to his own differences. Though Nemo's "lucky fin" originated with birth, and not accident (like Gil's scars), the two fish can nonetheless see themselves in each other. In the absence of Marlin, Gil becomes a semi-father figure.

In addition to Marlin and Gil, then, the other character in the film highlighted in a father role is Crush—a sea turtle "dude." This father allows his son, Squirt, to "find his own way." Whereas Marlin prefers that Nemo avoid certain challenges, and Gil presses Nemo through these challenges, Crush allows Squirt to face the challenges and adopt his own solution. It should be noted that these three fathers, either literally or by extension, are stereotypically white (even while being fish). Marlin is the Type A, overbearing and protective, uptight and anxious, class-privileged white father/fish. Crush is the Type B, go with the flow, it's all cool and will work itself out, "I'm your buddy," white father/fish. Gil is somewhere between Marlin and Crush. He directs Nemo, while he also grants him autonomy. His instructions to Nemo are delivered somewhat in the manner of a don (as discussed vis-à-vis *Shark Tale*), marking Gil in the stereotypical role of an Italian, mob-connected, white "godfather." In this respect, Gil's direction of Nemo is both that of a godfather (a mob-related Italian) and that of a "God father" (the stand-in father of an absent parent).

In fact, *Finding Nemo*, unlike *Shark Tale*, is a very "white" film. In addition to the whiteness of the characters (including the human characters, which are all white), the references beyond the film—to popular culture—are to other white characters. For instance, Bruce the shark "falls off the wagon" at one point in the film. He has been attending a support group for sharks trying to refrain from eating fish (in the spirit of Alcoholics Anonymous). However, Bruce's desires overcome him, and he chases after Marlin and Dory (Marlin's helpmate). As Bruce backs them into a corner, the threat of the situation is reinforced through Bruce's line, "Here's Brucey"—mimicking Jack Nicholson's line, "Here's Johnny," from the horror film *The Shining*. A second instance of underscored threat via popular culture is when the dentist's niece, Donna, enters his office. Donna is a known "bag shaker" to the aquarium fish; she killed her last "present" when she violently agitated its bag. As Donna makes her entrance, the well-known music to *Psycho* plays—Anthony Perkins's knife-wielding shower scene finding a parallel with Donna's anticipated bag-shaking office visit.

It is interesting that in *Finding Nemo*, as exemplified by Bruce and Donna, "threat" is coded as "white." From the perspective of a (white) mainstream audience, such racial coding would counter expectation—much as Marlin's lack of humor defies the standard expectation for a clown (fish) to be funny, or Nemo's ability to swim defies the standard expectation for a physically challenged individual (a small-finned fish) to be hindered. In a significant scene, however, in which Nemo (the newcomer) is initiated into the "eternal bonds of tankhood," the same audience precisely does find its expectations confirmed. In the initiation scene, Nemo is put through a series of challenges—he must swim through "the ring of fire," for example—amid chanting, a spewing "volcano," and notions of sacrifice. The fact that these representations are *not* white is clear, and Nemo must precisely maneuver through this terrain of "otherness" to become a member of the "brotherhood." Gil bestows the nickname "Sharkbait" upon Nemo and proclaims, "Sharkbait is one of us now." The use of racialized tropes as an initiation into (white) brotherhood is a maneuver worthy of note. Within this context, Nemo's proving himself capable of performing the initiation tasks (given his small fin) also serves to prove his whiteness; that is, he shows that he is able to "transcend" the superstition and "darkness" of the performed rites.

CONCLUSION

The main films discussed here, *Ice Age* and *Finding Nemo*, similar to ones discussed earlier in the text, such as *Dinosaur* and *Shark Tale*, suggest possibilities for non-mainstream and non-normative lessons about sexuality and gender, as well as family formation and configuration. In the end, however, such possibilities are reinscribed within a more normative frame and are ultimately recuperated from their straying positions. Thus, readings that foreground "transgression" or "queering" within contemporary films for children overlook, in our estimation, the cost of particular isolated moments. Specifically, such analyses neglect problematic messages delivered within the narrative, especially vis-à-vis race and ethnicity, that provide for their very possibility.

That is to say, while there might be a hope for something "different" residing within the messaging of certain animated films, "difference" in terms of gender/sexuality or family assumes the associated cost of exploiting problematic racialized tropes and narratives. Normalized and minimized story lines provide mainstream audiences a more comfortable encounter with moments of fleeting "difference"—moments that must be examined not only for their disruptive or resistant potential in one arena, but also for their reinscription of, and collusion with, problematic lessons in other arenas. While animated narratives might present certain alternatives to their audiences, their capacity to open up heterotopias, meaningful resistance, or oppositional spaces is ultimately undermined and limited by the "other" representations left intact and unproblematized within the story line—representations that inform the very appearance of the so-called alternatives. We turn, in the next chapter, to an account of the limits of politicized reception.

8

SCREENING RESISTANCE

Commodity Racism and Political Consumerism

Directors John Stevenson and Mark Osborne intended *Kung Fu Panda* to be a "love letter" to China, an animated "tribute to Chinese kung fu and the country's culture" (Zhang 2008). Given the film's success at the box office, a large number of Chinese were pleased with the American feature and its portrayal of their traditions, echoing sentiments of the state agency charged with reviewing the content of foreign movies, including their representations of China. *Kung Fu Panda*, seen by many filmgoers the world over as mere entertainment, became an important political platform, even before many in China had a chance to buy tickets. Performance artist and fashion designer Zhao Bandi, who has dubbed himself "Panda Man," invariably appearing in public with a stuffed panda cub as a hat, and centering his artistic creations around the iconic creature, protested the DreamWorks release. Although he had not seen *Kung Fu Panda*, Bandi called for a boycott of the movie and staged a public demonstration at its Chinese premier. Specifically, he charged that the film sought to exploit Chinese culture and misrepresented the nation and its heritage, and the timing of its release displayed insensitivity for the recent victims of a massive earthquake in Sichuan province. Steven Spielberg had insulted China through critical remarks about the nation's role in Darfur, withdrew as an advisor for the Beijing Olympics in protest, and generally reflected an anti-Chinese bias common in Hollywood.

It might be tempting to dismiss Bandi as an isolated voice, motivated by a desire for publicity, but his efforts did achieve a certain traction, forcing DreamWorks to delay the opening by nearly a week in Sichuan province. In addition, they point to the increasing importance of global audiences for animated films, while reflecting a rising cosmopolitanism and more nuanced articulations of national identity in the Chinese public sphere. Even more significant, Bandi's protest directs attention to a set of social movements and cultural practices emergent alongside of and often in response to the re-emergence of animated films over the past quarter of a century. Increasingly, audiences do not simply enjoy movies and happily consume ancillary products spun off from them; they make them vectors for social critiques and political actions.

Paralleling trends throughout consumer culture, animated films have become subject to what Michelle Micheletti (2003) and Micheletti and her colleagues (2004) have dubbed political consumerism (see also Jacobsen and Dulsrud 2007; Johnston 2008), a broad social movement through and against consumption directed at the means and ends of making, buying, and selling stuff. Much as the use of sweatshops prompted boycotts of apparel makers like Nike and a desire to benefit growers in underdeveloped countries gave rise to Fair Trade, film studios have also come under fire for their products. Importantly, in contrast with coffee cultivation and clothing manufacturing, which have fostered movements concerned with the means of production—particularly the unethical, if not exploitative, treatment of workers by multinational corporations—it is the content of animated films that has inspired action by (prospective) consumers against them. The rise of the political consumerism mirrors the resurgence of animated films. As a consequence, almost from the start of the new era in animation, individuals and organizations have mobilized against the messages conveyed by them.

In this chapter, we offer an overview of the politicized consumption of animated films during the past two decades. We analyze three forms of resistance, detailing the focus and impact of each distinct framework. We begin with a discussion of the racial politics of commodities and consumerism as well as the manner in which they have changed over the past four decades. Against this background, we include an account of the conservative critique of animated films, directed primarily at Disney, highlighting its preoccupation with context and its reliance on inversion and dehumanization to advance its agenda. Next, examining the boycott of *Shark Tale* called for by the Coalition against Racial, Religious and Ethnic Stereotyping, we interpret resistant readings that focus on stereotyping exclusively. Finally, we discuss a series of critical interventions that link text to context through their challenges to representations in films like *Aladdin*, *Pocahontas*, and *The Road to El Dorado*.

COMMODITY RACISM

In her classic work, *Imperial Leather*, McClintock (1995, 207–31) traces the multiplication of racism during the late nineteenth century. Specifically, she elaborates on the emergence of commodity racism, that is, the creation of racial registers beyond the then dominant language of scientific racism, allowing it to speak about the scope and significance of racial difference to new audiences formerly excluded by class, education, literacy, and gender. McClintock, furthermore, highlights the ways in which marketing and exhibitions emerged as consumer spectacles, seizing upon racial difference to inscribe narratives of difference and desire. Importantly, this novel economy of signs simultaneously rested upon prevailing understandings of gender and imperial expansion. Little better attests to this complex articulation, McClintock continues, than soap, which simultaneously knitted together domesticity, empire, and race. Selling soap meant selling race, gender, sexuality, and empire. In its initial formulation, particularly in the context of the then expanding United Kingdom, "[c]ommodity racism—in the specifically Victorian forms of advertising and photography, the imperial expositions and the museum movement—converted the narrative of imperial Progress into mass-produced *consumer spectacles*" (33, emphasis original).

Of course, commodity racism was neither restricted to Victorian Britain nor exclusively preoccupied with colonial cosmologies. In the context of the United States, during roughly the same period McClintock discusses, consumer culture certainly offered a language to work through the racial logics of imperial expansion, but of equal importance, blackness, the legacies of slavery, and racial rule proved fundamental to the exhibition, marketing, and circulation of commodities. In this context, its initial articulation—on myriad products, countless advertisements, and sundry mementoes and curios—commodity racism not only knitted together race and gender, public and private, self and other; as it established the boundaries, it also provided a framework for lived relations. Recent studies of consumer culture in the United States make plain that advertising and branding, no less than commodities and their uses, bound whites and blacks to particular roles and relations (see for instance, Hale 1999; Manring 1998). In the era following Reconstruction, the symbolic violence of the marketplace mirrored the lived terror and gruesome brutalities of Jim Crow. Specific commodities, such as Aunt Jemima pancake mix, emerged from vernacular culture (in this case minstrel shows) and crossed over as brand and world's fair exhibit to reinforce prevailing views of blacks (as servile, dependent, inferior), remind whites of their presumed superiority, justify exclusion, and reiterate nostalgic fantasies. Importantly, at the same time the commercialized imaginary was conjuring racial fantasies and escape routes for the white consumer, emergent spaces of consumption gave them material, erecting legal and practical barriers between whites and blacks, enforcing segregation in stores, hotels, beaches, and other public accommodations (as well as schools, buses, and housing). Sign and structure met and moved through the commodity form and its circulation. Importantly, it would be both the objects and sites of consumption which would later ground freedom struggles in the South: lunch counters and department stores, sports teams and pools, boycotts of products like Aunt Jemima, and a black arts movement that would in part animate itself through the visual interrogation of commodity racism.

BEFORE IDENTITY POLITICS

Song of the South (1946) provides an early example of commodity racism and responses to it by consumers (Cohen 2004). Noteworthy for its technological innovation that inserted animated characters and sequences into a live action film, the Disney feature centers on Uncle Remus and his relationship with a young, white, southern boy, to whom he relates folktales and imparts life lessons. Well in advance of the film's release, advisors, industry watchdogs, and advocacy groups, most notably the National Association for the Advancement of Colored People (NAACP), had highlighted its racist content and negative reception. Nevertheless, Disney did not listen to their concerns and opened it in segregated Atlanta. Although some critics lambasted the film for its demeaning treatment of African Americans and false portrait of the modern South, the film grossed more than $3 million and received much praise, including the Academy Award for Best Song for "Zip-a-Dee-Doo-Dah."

From the start, the NAACP criticized *Song of the South*. In a press release distributed on the film's opening day, executive secretary Walter White (quoted in Cohen 2004, 60–61) praised the "remarkable artistic merit" of the feature, but condemned its depiction of African Americans, history, and race relations:

> In an effort neither to offend audiences in the north or south, the production helps to perpetuate a dangerously glorified picture of slavery . . . [and] unfortunately gives an impression of an idyllic master-slave relationship which is a distortion of the facts.

The following month, the Theater Chapter of the National Negro Congress organized a demonstration outside of the Palace Theater in Times Square. One of the nearly twenty pickets, according to Cohen (2004, 61), declared "We fought for Uncle Sam, not Uncle Tom." And *Ebony* lamented that Disney had dismissed the concerns voiced during production, calling its readers to action: "It's about time that colored Americans wised up and went to work, counter-punching against the Hollywood that has given them perhaps their worst black eye in the opinion of white Americans" (quoted in Cohen 2004, 64). To prevent future harms, the magazine asserted that there was a need for a watchdog organization modeled after the National Decency League, which would monitor cinema for anti-black racism and facilitate boycotts and other political actions (Cohen 2004, 62).

Protests of *Song of the South*, reflective of the broader struggle for dignity, respectability, and humanity at the heart of the civil rights movement, sought to call attention to white power and the fictions that sustained it. Importantly, while not an immediate success, its sensibilities have reshaped the racial landscape: Disney, which later apologized, has never released the 1946 feature on video or DVD; the studio has edited other controversial characters out of previously released films, perhaps most famously, efforts to delete Sunflower the centaur from *Fantasia* (a character resembling a classic pickaninny who waits on more beautiful, white centaurs); and it has worked alongside competitors over the past quarter century to produce more multicultural films featuring "positive" portraits of cultural difference, save importantly, until the 2009 release of *The Princess and the Frog*, for African Americans (see the concluding chapter for more on this film).

THE NEW RACIAL POLITICS OF CONSUMPTION

This brief history of *Song of the South* reminds us of the centrality of animated film to racial identities and ideologies in the United States, while hinting at the long history of resistant readings. This history encourages a more complex assessment of the relationships between text and context.

A decade into the resurgence of animated film, journalist Jenn Shreve (1997) grappled with this complexity, providing a deceptively simple analysis:

Who would have thought it? The Walt Disney Company, once lauded as the last bastion of wholesome entertainment, is now being lambasted by a vocal but strange mix of Christians, Catholics, Muslims, family organizations, blind activists and fair-labor advocates—to name but a few. The fabled Mouse, they say, is a racist, sexist, gay-loving, visually challenged-bashing, Native American history-desecrating, anti-family, pro-sweatshop louse.

In a decade when intolerant left-wing political correctness cohabits with equally intolerant right-wing family-values mongering, it is difficult not to offend someone.

We want to propose that both the question and the answer are wrong: it mistakes self-promotion for veracity; it wrongly limits opposition to the present; and it reduces racism to a feeling—taking offense. The cultural politics Shreve describes, we suggest, are better understood as reflective of ideological shifts and structural realignments. Indeed, the reformulation of racism, the creation of new marketing languages, and the rise of political consumerism all have created a sociocultural context in which conservatives campaigning against equality and inclusion for gays and lesbians and indigenous people push back at relentless distortions of empire, seizing upon animated films as key to efforts to articulate political projects.

Changing material conditions have contributed to the crystallization of novel signifying practices for the connecting, conveying, and circulating of racial difference and social power. Important changes have occurred in the wake of the civil rights movement and the ongoing (racialized) wars at the heart of America: the war on drugs, the war on terror, and the culture wars. Understanding commodity racism today requires an acknowledgment that the victories secured more than a generation ago in struggles for racial freedom, social justice, and decolonization have become the contested terrain of neoconservative retrenchment. An awkward juxtaposition, to be sure, new racism does push us to recognize that social injustice and racial inequality fester in the United States, often in ways more pronounced and chronic than four decades ago, and provide tools to identify the terms and tactics that enliven, embody, and excuse it.

Patricia Hill Collins (2005) recognizes the shifting ideological contours, but draws our attention to their connection to material conditions. She concurs with Amy Ansell (1997) and Eduardo Bonilla-Silva (2003) that the centrality of culture to contemporary forms of racism is paramount:

> In prior periods in which biological theories were used to justify racist practices, racism and antiracism had a seemingly organic and oppositional relationship. One could either be *for* racism by believing that Blacks were biologically inferior and deserved the treatment they received or one could be *against* it by rejecting these beliefs and pointing to racial prejudice and institutional discrimination as more important in explaining Black disadvantage. These distinctions no longer hold for many White and Black Americans. Under the new color-blind racism that erases the color line, racism itself seems to have disappeared. (Collins 2005, 45)

To trace and prevent this disappearance, Collins identifies key structural issues: emergent global economic flows, transnational webs of power, and "new patterns of corporate organization," all of which perpetuate racial hierarchies without the rule of law or state violence (54). Of equal importance, she argues, mass media and consumer spectacle have proven central to the manufacture of consent and the reformulation of racism, in which according to Susan Willis (quoted in Lurry 1996, 166) race becomes little more than "a matter of style, something that can be put on or taken off at will." Worse, Hill continues, they "present hegemonic ideologies that claim that racism is over. They work to obscure the racism that does exist and they undercut antiracist protest" (54). Commodity racism, then, becomes a primary mediator in a global, post-industrial order, where the legacies and realities of racism make the system functional, meaningful, and profitable, but its presence must always be held under erasure, in which racial difference is desired and demonized, in which too often alternatives rather than being oppositional problems become absorbed as fads or fashions, readily accessible for co-optation and commodification.

Over the past four decades, the commodity form and the spectacles animating it have become among the primary arenas for the articulation of identity and the formulation of resistance. Although racialized communities had intermittently targeted commodities and their entanglements with racism in advance of the freedom struggles and decolonial movements that erupted after the Second World War, it was not until the late 1960s that consumption became fully politicized. For instance, African Americans pushed for and prompted changes to Aunt Jemima (Manring 1998), Chicanos pressured Frito-Lay to retire Frito Bandito (Noriega 2000, 28–50), and Native Americans began a campaign against disparaging sport mascots (King and Springwood 2001). The use of racialized images to market products became political, contributing to the articulation of new identity politics, which in turn laid the foundation for the reformulation, not the elimination, of commodity racism.

Thus commercial culture, particularly brands and advertisements, had emerged as a key site of opposition, a space in which to foster empowerment and articulate identity politics. Moreover, as such articulations focus on the visual rhetoric anchoring consumerism, images and stereotyping have centered these efforts, pushing the racial politics of consumption toward ugly images and, in turn, the identification of offended individuals. Corporations, in turn, work to contain dissent, and consciously or unconsciously direct attention away from racial structures and their unspoken center—whiteness.

Alongside familiar articulations of racialization and commodification, then, commodity racism itself has multiplied, now offering positive images that stress humanness and inclusion as they celebrate diversity and singularity. This turn has converged with the fragmentation of the consuming public into niche markets and in large part reflects a desire to cultivate "ethnic" markets. Commodity racism, which was formerly all about the projection of difference, makes a dual move in an era marked by multiculturalism: it simultaneously hails a broad, purportedly raceless audience and targets ethnic consumers, thus reinforcing racialized differences and their entanglements with power. According to Kim and Chung (2005, 88), multiculturalism enables media conglomerates "to profit off a multi-racial consumer base through greater inclusion while maintaining White male supremacy through . . . visual consumption." Or, as Giroux (1994) concludes, the logic of consumption in the age after race demands apolitical and essentialized images that project egalitarianism and equivalence as they erase the legacies of white supremacy.

A MEASURE OF SUCCESS

In 2006, *Entertainment Weekly* named *Aladdin* one of the twenty-five most controversial movies of all time. The Disney classic received this dubious distinction not because of the clear ways in which it reiterated Orientalist clichés in the immediate aftermath of the First Gulf War (Macleod 2003; Wise 2003), but rather in large part because of the efforts of the Arab-American Anti-Discrimination Committee (ADC) to educate the public about the stereotypes and misrepresentations central to the 1992 film. It prefers fantasies of an exotic and alien generic Arabia as a backdrop for a formulaic romance to a culturally accurate and historically anchored story in an actual time and place. Moreover, according to the ADC, the film uses easily discernible features to link racial and moral distinctions:

> The film's light-skinned lead characters, Aladdin and Jasmine, have Anglicized features and Anglo-American accents. This is in contrast

to the other characters who are dark-skinned, swarthy and villain-
ous—cruel palace guards or greedy merchants with Arabic accents
and grotesque facial features. (Wingfield and Karaman 1995)

Worse, the catchy soundtrack of the film plays off disturbing
stereotypes. The opening song, "Arabian Nights," originally included the following lyrics:

> Oh, I come from a land
> From a faraway place
> Where the caravan camels roam
> Where they cut off your ear
> If they don't like your face
> It's barbaric, but hey it's home

Echoing the efforts of the NAACP nearly fifty years before, the ADC
launched a public campaign that questioned the media giant and its
depictions of difference. In contrast with its earlier indifference to
the concerns of advocacy groups and the more recent efforts at denial, Disney opted to forge a compromise of sorts that would require
limited alteration, even as it publicly affirmed a commitment to diversity. Specifically, it changed lyrics in the title song and agreed to
consult more fully with the Arab American community.

> Oh, I come from a land
> From a faraway place
> Where the caravan camels roam
> Where it's flat and immense
> And the heat is intense
> It's barbaric, but hey it's home

This half measure allowed Disney and much of its audience to
picture Arabs as barbaric others, but without the overt and vio-

lent tones. The success of the ADC, if that is the right way to phrase it, marks the beginning of a newly politicized era of consumption in which individuals and organizations associated with the Religious Right and anti-racist activists would openly use animated films to advance their agendas, albeit through very different strategies.

BOYCOTT TO BUYCOTT

In the mid-1990s, Disney became a focal point in the ongoing culture wars. Although its extension of benefits to same-sex couples, annual hosting of "Gay Days" at Disney World, distribution of R-rated movies via Miramax, and television programming, particularly *Ellen*, were causes for much concern among the rising Religious Right, animated films played an important role in neoconservative efforts to politicize the consumption of all things Disney.

Beginning in 1996, organizations like the American Family Association, the Southern Baptist Convention, and the American Life League and countless individuals invested in the cultural agenda of fundamentalist Christianity began advocating for a boycott of Disney. The multimedia conglomerate became a front in the culture wars because of its contributions to the erosion of family values and degradation of public decency as well as its visible support of what those on the Religious Right have termed "the homosexual agenda." The boycott persisted for nearly nine years, when advocates ended it, claiming a modicum of victory and a need to address other, more pressing issues.

Advocates of the Disney boycott seized upon recent animated features to advance their position, but did so in rather unexpected ways. In fact, at first blush, films like *The Little Mermaid*, *The Lion King*, *Beauty and the Beast*, and *Pocahontas* appear, as we have suggested previously in this text, to support heterosexual romance, family, individualism, and other core American values. To politicize these movies, fundamentalist critics literally read context into the text, projecting their preoccupations onto them.

First, viewers found subliminal messages in Disney's animated revival. For instance, the American Life League purported to find an inappropriate scene in *The Lion King*:

> Forlorn over the death of his father, the young lion [Simba] flops dejectedly on the ground near the edge of a cliff. The result, offended viewers say, is a cloud of dust particles that swirls and swoops to form the word "sex," and then quickly fades away. (Smith 1995)

In *The Little Mermaid*, others claimed, the pastor at the wedding ceremony becomes aroused. Meanwhile, *Aladdin*, critics say, tells teenagers during a pivotal scene to "take off your clothes" (Bannon 1995). And, in a deviation from the historical record, they argue, Disney suppresses the fact that Pocahontas converted to Christianity. These hidden and largely sexualized messages caused many fundamentalists to rethink an institution they had once revered: "I felt as if I had entrusted my kids to pedophiles. . . . It's like a toddler introduction to porn" (Bannon 1995).

Second, the Disney boycott hinged on identifying gays and lesbians at Disney and linking them to the production of animated films. One website advocating the boycott, citing an article in *Buzz* magazine, lamented that a plurality of employees at Disney might be gays or lesbians. It then proceeds to highlight one of the producers of *The Lion King* "as an open homosexual" and asserting the same about an animator who played a leading role in illustrating *Beauty and the Beast* ("Disney Boycott" 1996).

Both of these techniques, of course, have more in common with witch hunts designed to purify the social body of perceived transgressors than they do with raising healthy and happy children, promoting family, or enhancing cultural life. They allow believers in the de facto national religion to simultaneously position themselves as victims and their values as imperiled even as they stigmatize and dehumanize people long marginalized, persecuted, and demeaned in public life. Importantly, a concern for the harms associated with actual social problems has no place in the cosmology of those advancing the Disney boycott. From this perspective, the problem with *Pocahontas* rests not in its erasure of empire, dispossession, and genocide, nor its distortions of indigenous peoples, but in the deletion of one biographical fact. Only those cloaked in racial privilege and settled in their relation to conquest could remain so silent about these issues.

Little had changed in 2005, when the boycott came to an official end. In a press release, American Family Association president Tim Wildmon asserted,

> We feel after nine years of boycotting Disney we have made our point. . . . Boycotts have always been a last resort for us at AFA, and Disney's attitude, arrogance and embrace of the homosexual lifestyle gave us no choice but to advocate a boycott of the company these last few years. (American Family Association 2005)

He felt the boycott had produced "positive things." Michael Eisner had left Disney and Miramax had separated from the multimedia conglomerate. Moreover, Wildmon noted that Disney had embraced Christianity, reaching out to the "religious community" and producing films, like *The Lion, the Witch and the Wardrobe*, which in their view affirmed Christian values. In many respects, Disney transformed the boycott into a buycott, in which fundamentalist Christians became a niche market, rather than an oppositional group refusing to consume its products. In doing so, however, they reinforced the core and its reactionary backlash against hard-won victories of people of color, women, and gays and lesbians.

AGAINST STEREOTYPES

Even as the boycott of Disney by the American Family Association, the Southern Baptist Convention, and other groups associated with the Religious Right neared exhaustion, the National Coalition against Racial, Religious and Ethnic Stereotyping (CARRES) initiated a campaign against DreamWorks' animated feature *Shark Tale*. CARRES brought together a number of social and cultural organizations, primarily those concerned with the Italian American community and its heritage, including National Italian American Foundation, National Organization of Italian American Women, Order Sons of Italy in America, Girabaldi Guard, American Italian Defense Fund, and the Italian American Task Force on Defamation, to boycott DreamWorks and its corporate partners, specifically Burger King, Krispy Kreme, Coca-Cola, and Cheerios. The coalition, in common with the neoconservative critics of Disney, stressed the dangers the animated feature posed to children. Specifically, it sought to fight back against what it termed an "assault on our children," asserting that the key issue was "about propagandizing children, especially OUR children and grandchildren, in a movie that should not even have ethnic overtones." Not unlike the NAACP half a century before, CARRES had consulted with the filmmakers in advance, but their efforts to "de-Italianize" the picture proved unsuccessful. As a consequence, *Shark Tale* recycled clichéd images of Italian Americans as mobsters, ruled by their emotions, prone to violence, involved in criminal activities, and identifiable through their use of dialect and broken English. In adapting "the 'mafia' theme" for children, DreamWorks and Spielberg, according to CARRES, had shown themselves to be bigots, producing "propaganda" like "Hollywood used on African Americans and Nazis used on Jews." Much as imagery stigmatized these groups in the past, they continue, *Shark Tale* threatened to reinforce an established linkage in the popular imaginary: "[m]ost people see someone with an Italian name as 'ethnic' rather than 'all-American.'" In targeting ethnic stereotypes, moreover, the coalition asserted it was fighting for equality and inclusion: "We cannot allow our children to be subjected to this second-class citizenship."

Despite their efforts, CARRES's push to politicize *Shark Tale* and mount a boycott of DreamWorks and its corporate partners had little, if any, impact on the film's revenues and did not found a new movement around imagery and its effects. Instead, CARRES appears to have dissolved shortly after the feature's release, even though the Internet still archives its efforts (see http://www.osia.org/public/commission/shark_tale.asp). For its part, DreamWorks suggested the animated feature contained nothing negative and was meant, like *Shrek*, to be a parody of the very images that troubled CARRES (van Gelder 2004).

CARRES's interpretation of *Shark Tale* and the organization's failed push to politicize consumption offer important insights, however. Focusing exclusively on stereotyping, it limited its intervention to an engagement with a text and its injurious content. Its superficial reading of the film isolates it from history and context. To be sure, the coalition's pamphlet makes reference to a tradition of cinematic misrepresentation, invoking the then popular *Sopranos* series specifically, but it does not ground its critique in a discussion of exclusion and exploitation. It does not connect signification to structure in any meaningful way, in part, one imagines, because even as *Shark Tale* foregrounds the ethnicity of Italian Americans, making their whiteness more specific, it does not in any real way imperil their claims to whiteness. Indeed, one of the troubling features of the CARRES campaign is its appropriation of the rhetoric of anti-racist struggle and legacies of the civil rights movement to defend already secured claims to white privilege. Piana (2004) summarizes the awkwardness of the coalition's approach and location:

> CARRES was not established to right the historic wrong of racism in the Italian American community, rather to end the ongoing stereotyping of Italians in American popular culture. Herein lies the problem. While the stereotype of the Italian mobster certainly is prevalent, it is hardly the cutting edge of racism. Some stereotypes have higher consequences than others.
>
> During World War II, 600,000 Italian Americans were put on travel restriction and thousands of fishermen had their boats confiscated out of the belief they were loyal to Mussolini. But today, Italians are not stopped by the police because of their skin color or prevented from flying because of their last names. Racial profiling is however the ongoing reality for people of color today.

Silence on these histories and these legacies undermines any efforts to build a dynamic movement against racism. In fact, it is not at all clear that CARRES wishes to battle racism per se, for while it readily identifies the false images energizing *Shark Tale*, it attributes these to "financial greed," which it reads as a social "disease." Furthermore, while manifesting great outrage about the image of Italian Americans, it neither lent its voice to critical commentaries on other contemporary films and their portrayals of blacks, Latinos, and/or indigenous peoples, nor made any connection in its own analysis of *Shark Tales* to the manner in which misrepresentations in this film resonated with (and differed from) images of other ethnic groups in past or present animated features. A final measure of the racial politics of the *Shark Tale* boycott can be found in the coalition itself. Dominated by Italian American heritage and cultural and social organization, it was an all-white coalition, as only groups beyond the Italian American community to join were the Polish American Congress, the American-Arab Anti-Discrimination Committee, and the Arab American Institute, representing similarly disparaged and marginal white ethnic groups. Absent were longstanding groups committed to social justice and the struggle against racism, including the NAACP, National Council of La Raza, and the Anti-Defamation League—which all opted not to participate in the boycott.

ANTI-RACIST PROJECTS

Although lacking the size, scope, or resources of either the neoconservative movement against Disney or the boycott of Dream-Works sponsored by CARRES, individuals and organizations concerned about racism and often its connection to sexism have loudly voiced their opposition to animated films that use cultural difference as a prop, setting, or story line. *Aladdin* is an early example, followed shortly thereafter by *Pocahontas*, and more recently by *The Road to El Dorado* and the still unreleased *The Princess and the Frog*. Calls to boycott these films regularly appear online in discussion forums or via e-mail, but less frequently congeal as mass movements. Instead, to date efforts to advance antiracist projects against animated films have remained largely decentered, reflecting the atomism of contemporary consumer society, the anemic state of progressive, counter-hegemonic social movements, and the prevailing abstract liberalism that renders such efforts a matter of taste, one choice among several equally viable options. Nevertheless, in the fragmented struggle to foreground the racial politics of animated film consumption, one can glimpse the outline of critical literacy that holds out the promise of injecting a vernacular anti-racism into the broader landscape of political consumerism. One of the better examples can be found in opposition to *The Road to El Dorado*.

Both the Mexika Eagle Society and the Mexica Movement called for a boycott of DreamWorks in the fall of 2000, as did a number of individuals. The commentaries echoed other efforts to politicize animated films: false and hurtful images pervade the film, which in turn pose a threat to young people. Importantly, this was not the end of the analysis, but merely a foundation for a more complex and politically charged engagement with representation, history, and power. Indeed, efforts to politicize *The Road to El Dorado* share a tendency to place text in context, as the interpretation connects stereotypes to structures, and correct errors with facts. Given the setting and story line of the film this means that critical readings by activists openly confront topics typically taboo in conversations about popular culture and collective memory, conquest, and genocide.

For instance, speaking for the Mexica Movement, Olin Tezcatlipoca (2000) compared the film to a fictional story for children produced in the aftermath of the Holocaust that would romanticize the perpetrators (the Nazis) and their deeds in the contexts of a romantic comedy set amid the former concentration camps. To be sure, this comparison is vulgar and at a deeper level works against its own politics, but it illustrates the extremes to which one must go to make the context visible. Against the background of this hyperbole, Tezcatlipoca resituates the Spanish quest for El Dorado in the context of conquest, the search for material resources, and the mass death of native peoples.

Similarly, physician Sara Vasquez (2000), in an open letter to Steven Spielberg and Edward James Olmos (producer and star of the film respectively), offers a biting critique of the film and indicates her intention to encourage everyone she knows (and presumably all of the readers of the letter) to boycott the film. Her analysis is more nuanced that Tezcatlipoca's. She begins:

> I saw "The Road to El Dorado" yesterday with my nephews and niece, at a sneak preview in the Chicago area. I left the theater

feeling sick and angry about the horrible racist and sexist stereotypes depicted in this cartoon. I had to talk with my children for
an hour so they could understand that what they had seen did not
reflect any past nor current reality.

Having established the harm (misrepresentation), the impact
(anger and trauma), and the imperiled (her niece and nephews),
she continues to further enumerate the representational trans-
gressions of the film:

> As a Mexican-American woman, I felt that the portrayal of the In-
> dian characters in the movie was universally degrading to my gen-
> der and ethnicity; from the vacantly-expressioned childlike towns-
> people, to the scantily-clad loose-moraled heroine, to the
> bloodthirsty conniving priest, all portrayed the worst stereotypes
> that continue to hurt Indigenous and mestizo people today. While
> the Spanish heroes displayed full ranges of intellect, expression
> and physical ability, the Indians were all monofaceted, ignorant,
> sheeplike, and helpless. The religion of the Indians was shown as
> evil, fantastic, manipulative, and disconnected from the people,
> and by the end of the cartoon had apparently been thrown down
> by the noble Europeans.

To Vasquez, these images are all the worse because of the ways
in which they contribute to the affirmation of false histories—
"perpetuat[ing] the myth the Europeans 'discovered' America"
and that nothing of value was here prior to Europeans—and the
erasure of the structural violence, cultural trauma, and mass
death. Importantly, Vasquez highlights something else crucial to
the alternative literacy at the heart of anti-racist projects (that is
found in the other efforts to politicize the consumption of *The
Road to El Dorado*): intersectional interpretation. As our own
analysis of the film asserted early the two cannot be disentangled,
and Sanchez underscores this point, nicely grounding it in her
own experience and positionality.

Ultimately, as the Mexika Eagle Society noted, "This [protest] is about human dignity and having respect for the history and traditions of others." Here their words echo those of the NAACP nearly fifty years before, attesting to the fundamental force of commodity racism even in an age supposedly after race, the persistence of struggle against it, and frustratingly, the limited impact they have had—then and now.

CONCLUSION

As should be clear, political consumerism is not in and of itself a liberatory practice. Bringing popular texts like animated films into political struggles energizes social movements, allowing them to heighten visibility while clearing a space in which they can speak clearly about core concerns. Indeed, the Religious Right projected its agenda and the broader context of the cultural wars onto Disney and its animated features, intensifying its pursuit of nostalgic and dehumanizing politics that targeted difference, particularly what it read as deviant and prurient and embodied by gays and lesbians. No less troubling, if less reactionary, was CARRES's move to combat ethnic stereotyping out of context and isolated from racism. Rather than promise emancipation, their project sought unencumbered access to whiteness and the privileges that come with it. Like the Religious Right, the Italian American groups composing CARRES used the language of injury to formulate identity and advance an agenda—a rather cynical poaching of the rhetoric of the civil rights movement that their political projects repudiate. Politicized consumption has the potential to unsettle the animation of difference in film, and its dangerous liaisons with prevailing force fields are those interventions that place texts in contexts, offering counter-readings that make linkages between signification and structures. Lacking to date have been an intersectional approach and the forging of coalitions, elements that might lay the foundation for a more dynamic cultural politics.

Although political consumerism has focused attention on the ways in which animated films misrepresent race and history, thereby perpetuating the structural marginalization and systematic disadvantage of non-whites, the call for boycotts has had a negligible impact on the production and consumption of animated films. In part, this undoubtedly derives from the tendency to view entertainment as apolitical and inconsequential—it is just a movie, which intends to be a fun diversion—as well as an inability to engage the legacies of empire and the persistence of racial, sexual, and gendered injustices. Perhaps more importantly, it says something more fundamental about the political economy of animating difference: consumption is erratic, individual, uneven, and ultimately all about choice in a marketplace in which truth, race, justice, and inclusion have become a matter of taste and style. Within this context, community, identity, experience, and history become mere commodities; in contrast, production remains firmly within the grasp of cultural elites, who are content to recycle slightly modified cultural myths central to collective memory and social relations so long as they turn a profit. Media literacy may be a path toward more empowered citizens and engaged consumers, but this will always remain a reactive strategy. More consequential, then, it is precisely the means of production that must be politicized and claimed by activists if they hope to materialize a truly emancipatory, anti-racist, anti-(hetero)sexist cultural politics. While the cost, size, and scope of contemporary Hollywood features may make us dubious of the prospects of such projects, at least three developments suggest creative alternatives. First, following Judith Halberstam and pushing our argument toward its end, authoring narratives that decouple themselves from the engines of romance and family may clear a space for the articulation of a more open and inclusive cinema. Second, marginalized communities have found in other genres of animation meaningful alternatives: expressive forms like comic books, art, and performance offer meaningful examples of their counterhegemonic potential. Finally, it may be in the new media, in spite of the digital divide, that an alternative cinema may fully be realized. Websites and digital technology already show some promise toward these ends. In the end, as important as politicized consumption has been, we hold our hope out for the crystallization of a repoliticized production.

9

COMING ATTRACTIONS

As we conclude this book, Disney is scheduled to release the animated feature *The Princess and the Frog* in December 2009. At first glance, the film appears to be yet another Disney-fied tale involving a princess. Disney, however, attempts to counter the impression that this film represents business as usual by claiming that *The Princess and the Frog* is a "new" incarnation of the fairy tale, loosely based on the 2002 novel *The Frog Princess* by E. D. Baker, and includes a modern-day interpretation. In the words of Disney: the film is "an animated comedy set in the great city of New Orleans" and provides "a modern twist on a classic tale, featuring a beautiful girl named Tiana, as well as a frog prince who desperately wants to be human again, and a fateful kiss that leads them both on a hilarious adventure through the mystical bayous of Louisiana" (Disney.com 2009). Although they do not clearly articulate the details of the so-called modern twist, we could speculate that Disney intends to reference the fact that the princess herself turns into a frog after kissing the prince frog, rather than the prince frog turning into a handsome and available human prince (which would be the audience's expectation, based on similar folkloric tales). Moreover, in contrast with the context-less far, far away kingdoms in which princesses usually live (satirized in the *Shrek* franchise), this princess comes to life and the plot develops in a specific place and time: New Orleans, Louisiana, in the 1920s.

Disney might not promote the twist as being due to the fact that Princess Tiana is black, since Disney princesses and the stories they embody are supposed to be timeless (which can be read as a coded description for raceless and without context—despite Arabian Princess Jasmine, and Native American Princess Pocahontas). However, *The Princess and the Frog* is a story in which the princess is in fact black, the setting is New Orleans, and the time period is the 1920s. These elements are important to consider at this historical juncture. According to the film's producer, Peter Del Vecho, those who worked on *The Princess and the Frog* "[felt] a great responsibility to get this right. Every artistic decision [was] carefully thought out." He adds, "[T]he idea for a black princess came about organically. The producers wanted to create a fairy tale set in the United States and centered on New Orleans, with its colorful past and deep musical history" (Barnes 2009).

The trailers and posters for the film present a regal Tiana dressed in a way similar to Disney's white princesses: in a princess-worthy, light green (almost white) gown, pearls, and a tiara. Given the problematic history of racial representations involving Disney and other companies producing animated films, it would be understandable to adopt a stance celebrating the "arrival" (or more accurately, Disney's depiction) of a black princess. Such celebratory positions have indeed heralded the advent of a black princess as either a positive event in keeping with current trends (including the election of the first black U.S. president, and the "arrival" of the first black first lady), or a cutting-edge act by Disney (affording the view that Disney did not have to give us a black princess, yet it did, and this is cause for celebration). For instance, in a news blurb regarding the film posted on its website, Black Entertainment Television (BET) states the following: "Historically, Walt Disney Studio has had a less than savory record regarding images of African Americans in its animated works, so it was with great excitement that the Black community received the media giant's first Black princess" (BET News 2009). Similarly, in an interview with CNN, entertainment director at *Essence* magazine, Cori Murray, stated, "Finally, here is something that all little girls, especially young black girls, can embrace" (Barnes 2009).

We wish we could share this optimism and enthusiasm. As scholars committed to critical engagements with racialization and sexualization and concerned about the manner in which such images shape the understandings, identities, and possibilities of young people, especially young women (of color), we find in *The Princess and the Frog* not cause for hope, but a reiteration of white racial (hetero)sexist frames. Moreover, although we have not seen Disney's new princess tale, our attention to promotional materials and public discussions has led us to believe that the film encapsulates the central argument and interpretive themes of *Animating Difference*. Thus, in this final chapter, we reflect on this coming attraction in relation to our efforts to deconstruct the resurgence of animated films over the past two decades. In particular, we highlight the fundamental elements of white racial (hetero)sexist framing: (a) false positivity—seemingly positive images that in actuality denigrate difference, (b) disavowal, (c) valorizing whiteness, (d) whitewashing history, (e) imperial longings/empire, (f) citizenship, (g) socialization, (h) heterosexual magic, and

(i) superficial/contained alternatives. We endeavor to outline the scope and significance of white racial (hetero)sexist frames, while reflecting on the future of animation and critical scholarship devoted to it.

FALSE POSITIVITY

With *The Princess and the Frog*, Disney has returned to blackness, more than fifty years after *Song of the South*. Although one might wonder why it took the entertainment conglomerate so long to take up the central racial question haunting life in the United States—the color line dividing whites and blacks—the move certainly marks a major change. Previously, African Americans have been all but absent from animated cinema, appearing as sidekicks and often speaking in stereotypic "Black English." In place of the ugliness projected onto the crow in *Dumbo* through negative stereotypes, *The Princess and the Frog* renders blackness beautiful, appealing, as the commentators quoted above attest, to whites as well as blacks. Even if Tiana spends much of the movie in the body of a frog, rather than that of a young African American woman, it is clear that we have entered a new era, or, perhaps better said, are witnessing the most powerful articulation of its reigning ideologies. Representations of difference in consumer culture, polite society, and public discourse have been recoded, sanitized, and written in a positive register, and as a consequence, celebration has prevailed over demonization. This shift in white racial (hetero)sexist frames has not been complete or uncontested, but, within animated cinema and beyond, its prevalence poses at least three problems: (1) positive stereotypes are still stereotypes which present distorted and dehumanizing renderings; (2) the values at the heart of the dominant framing (such as beauty standards), rather than those of say African

Americans, delimit what is good, worthy, and acceptable; and (3) positivity allows audiences to forget the difference that difference makes and enjoy the delusion of a society after racism and (hetero)sexism. The resurgence of animated films follows the reworking of difference as diversity and enacts the languages of multiculturalism. Throughout the reborn genre, as our foregoing analyses have noted, there has been an accentuation of the positive. From *Kung Fu Panda* (drawn as a love letter to China) to *Pocahontas* (depicting a beautiful princess who is smart, strong, and in harmonious relations with those around her), the "other" is frequently pictured as desirable, worthy, even human. Importantly, it is precisely gender and heterosexuality that often energize positivity in these features: the beauty, if not sex appeal, of leading ladies from Chel and Pocahontas to Jasmine and EVE attract the gaze, enable connection, and soften difference to interchangeable styles. Of course, what makes them appealing, beautiful, and consumable is the manner in which they fit established (white, heterosexual) beauty standards, which makes one wonder how positive these images are in actuality. And whatever they project through flattery remains a flat stereotype that doubles the denial of humanity, simplifying the Powhatan, Chinese, Arab, or Incan other in perverse ways. Finally, despite all of the pretty pictures and good feelings in contemporary animated features, ugly images still persist—such as the hyenas in *The Lion King* and the Rastafarian jellyfish in *Shark Tale*. Even as these images fade from the screen and more prominent and appealing representations replace them, white racial (hetero)sexist frames dictate the production and reception of difference, so it is not so much that we have shed bad baggage on a progressive path toward enlightenment, but rather that means of creation and meanings expressed have been reframed to mediate novel social circumstances and meditate upon emergent cultural concerns.

DISAVOWAL

Making use of anthropomorphized racial representations and racial signifiers, *The Princess and the Frog* presents us with other dilemmas as well, particularly ones involving the trope of the princess and commodity racism. That is, we could say that the problem with the black princess is not so much in the black part of the character but in the princess part. Given our society's disavowal of hierarchical social positioning (as social scientists have repeatedly pointed out, regardless of their actual social standing, Americans tend to see themselves as "middle class"), the image of an American princess seems anachronistic, as monarchies represent an unrelatable sort of social and economic structure to Americans. Her blackness, in contrast, allows for another sort of disavowal, that of the lingering significance of race. Indeed, the historical setting is an important means of distancing difference, allowing audiences to recognize and even name racism as a problem without having to think ill of the present. After all, they are enjoying a film with a black protagonist who is beautiful and makes them happy. Throughout this book, we have drawn attention to similar strategies of disavowal in animated cinema. In addition to positive images springing from the multicultural imagination and the distance provided by history, animated films, in spite of the projection of obvious differences, insist on a universal humanness: we are all the same, sharing similar desires, feelings, and motivations.

While *Pocahontas* points to difference as the cause of conflict between the Powhatan and English colonists, equally important has been the invocation of heterosexual love—a love deemed universal. Indeed, animated films propose that desire and attraction across boundaries have the capacity to resolve differences and misunderstandings. *Pocahontas* again exemplifies this pattern, as do *The Road to El Dorado*, the *Shrek* franchise, and *Madagascar:*

Escape 2 Africa. Moreover, these films favor erasure as a means of avoiding the uncomfortable realities they fictionalize, ranging from the disappearing of Africans from films set in Africa to the sanitizing of context (no genocide follows conquest). Finally, as we discuss below, animated films incorporate unruly, even transgressive, elements, only to contain or redirect them.

VALORIZING WHITENESS

At first blush, *The Princess and the Frog* appears to be valorizing blackness, elevating it as it alters its place and presentation in animated cinema. While we cannot fully judge the film without viewing it first, it seems clear that like Pocahontas and Jasmine, Tiana takes shape through the white gaze, particularly the norms of attractiveness and body composition directing it. As a consequence, we have real worries about its capacity to transform blackness and the landscape of animated films. Indeed, we see in the film's trailer a familiar, if more subtle, restatement of the racialized facts of life: whiteness as center, norm, and limit, which its "others" orbit, supplement, and bring into sharper focus. Indeed, as we have sought to clarify throughout *Animating Difference*, guided by white racial (hetero)sexist frames, films in this genre reflect and reinforce white identities, ideologies, and interpretations. With few exceptions that center on royals of color, animated films focus on whites. For instance, *WALL-E* cannot imagine a future in which whites do not dominate society or have a right to colonize; similarly, *Pocahontas, Spirit,* and *The Road to El Dorado* underscore that history is white, shaped by the actions of Europeans and Americans. Even when subject to critique, beliefs and behaviors associated with whiteness (proper speech patterns, hard work, family life, and the good life) are rendered as normal, and typically as superior.

Although often universalized, whiteness is also particularized in animated cinema. As we discussed in chapter 8, the animated film *Cars* offers the audience a clear example of racialized anthropomorphism: in the film, each car is racialized. What becomes interesting about this particular film is the heavily nuanced way in which whiteness is portrayed. That is, while cars "of color" are one-dimensional and flatly "of color" (one obviously Mexican, one obviously black, etc.), white cars have a variety of characteristics: we see the spoiled young white male (Lightning McQueen); the successful female lawyer turned small business owner and advocate of Radiator Springs (Sally); the small-town born and bred, low-educated male (Mater); the ex-military male (Sarge); the former race car male champion (Sheriff); the hippy, stuck-in–the-'60s male (Van); and even the white male immigrant (Luigi), among many other representations of whiteness.

The investment in and valorizing of whiteness is not always presented in a straightforward manner, however. As we discussed in chapter 4, at times narratives in animated films weave whiteness and citizenship together. We are curious to see how Disney presents the blackness of the princess in *The Princess and the Frog*, though if past films are any indication, we can predict that her blackness will be drowned by her royal status (which will become a whitening or mainstreaming tool). That is to say, a black princess will become just a princess (in a world where princesses are white or honorary white members), especially given that her frog Prince Charming seems to be white, and given that (as we discuss below) we doubt she will be placed within the horrors of black history in the United States.

WHITEWASHING HISTORY

Setting *The Princess and the Frog* in the past distances audiences from the realities of racism today and distorts the historical legacies of exploitation and exclusion. In fact, it is difficult to imagine a more awkward context than the Jim Crow South for the story of an African American princess. On the surface, the depiction of a black princess dressed in royal regalia and sporting a tiara in 1920s Louisiana poses obvious problems. After all, the 1920s are still painfully close to 1865 and are in the midst of segregation practices (which were part of Louisiana's law) and lynchings (which took place in Louisiana). The idea of a black princess within that context does raise some important questions; for example, where does she and/or her royal lineage originate? and what does her tiara (usually a symbol of wealth and power) symbolize? These are important questions to consider in trying to understand the context for a black princess in the U.S. South, which Disney may very well attempt to market in the same way that it has packaged its contextless white princesses, or its almost contextless princesses of color. As we have addressed throughout this book, Disney and other studios have notoriously ignored, erased, or rewritten history.

In a very real sense, during the preceding two decades, animated cinema has restaged white myths about the past, recasting popular memory to address emergent social problems, while maintaining a pronounced fidelity to the central fictions of (white) American ideologies and identities. As discussed most fully in chapter 4, films in this genre have whitewashed history, making it more simple, sanitized, and consumable by whiting out much of the messiness associated with imperialism and cultural difference. Whereas films set in Africa erase indigenous peoples, render its landscapes timeless, and underscore white supremacy, features set in North America have acknowledged the inevitable, if uncomfortable, force of colonization, simultaneously offering a soft critique of past practices and perceptions, even as they ground national origins and identities in (relation to) indigeneity. As a consequence, animated cinema has redrawn the mythic consciousness of settler society. Recolonizing blackness, *The*

Princess and the Frog appears primed to do something similar for the dominant framings of race in the United States.

IMPERIAL LONGINGS/EMPIRE

In the world of animated films empire and its grasp are represented by multiculturalist story-(re)telling. The retelling of the conquest of the Americas in *The Road to El Dorado, Pocahontas,* and *Spirit,* along with the retelling of the Hunan invasion of China in *Mulan,* the representation of Inca culture in *The Emperor's New Groove,* the representation of native Hawaiians in *Lilo and Stitch,* and the "taking" of the "Dark Continent" in the *Madagascar* franchise, *The Lion King,* and *Tarzan,* for instance, give us an idea of the workings of empire through multicultural representations. As we have argued throughout *Animating Difference,* representations of both people and animals in these films are problematic on many counts, but even more problematic is the fact that the stories do not belong to the indigenous peoples of the Americas, or the Chinese, or the native Hawaiians, or the Africans. These stories belong to those who have the power to tell/sell them: animated film studios. According to Michael Hardt and Antonio Negri (2001), empire includes economic, social, political, and juridical aspects. We would add that empire includes aspects of popular culture (including animated films) that are used to justify and even at times glorify and legitimate the economic, social, political, and juridical aspects. This is why a black princess, in our view, makes no significant difference within the larger frame of tales justifying ideologies.

CITIZENSHIP

Similar to the tropes of empire and multiculturalism, the trope of citizenship is used to tell stories, this time stories of belonging. As we discussed in chapter 6, in many of these animated films, citizenship is embedded within constructions of femininity. We are also clear that these constructions are ideological, noting that their importance rests on the fact that they instruct children about two important things: normalcy and morality. They also allow children to develop ideas about themselves as both legal (or rightful) and cultural citizens. Animated films grant cultural citizenship to those who "belong" and belonging means advancing the ideologies embedded within mainstream (white) culture. Animated constructions of citizenship then make us wonder, how will a black princess gain her American (cultural and legal) citizenship? That is to say, what kind of ideologies will she have to advance in order to "become" a citizen?

SOCIALIZATION

Every aspect of our discussion in this conclusion connects with socialization, for each aspect is conveying/reinforcing ideologies, ways of looking at the world, and messages about right, wrong, and how to act generally and under specific circumstances. But it is, perhaps, in representations of gender and gender roles that we gain the best insight into the relationship between socialization and animated films. As we discussed in earlier chapters, recent animated films seem to portray more nuanced gender roles than earlier (Disney) films. Though gender roles and masculinity for male characters have not changed drastically since Prince Charming kissed Snow White, female gender roles have (and thus femininity has) undergone substantive modifications, including the fact that female characters seem to have more agency. In addition, animated femininity seems to be more assertive, and we cannot forget that female characters have also been highly sexualized (via body shape, clothing, and banter) in recent portrayals.

What is interesting to us is that agency notwithstanding, "girls" in animated films still conform to and abide by the old rules: a girl, even an independent, self-sufficient, and/or sexually playful girl must bow down to heteronormativity by either finding her man (as in the case of grown-up "girls" like Mulan) or by finding comfort and/or purpose in heteronormativity (as in the case of "less grown" girls like Lilo). Similarly, we can never have a princess (white, black, Native American, or Arab) without a prince.

HETEROSEXUAL MAGIC

As we have noted throughout, animated films rely upon incorporation of heterosexuality in order to propel their stories and reinforce their themes. In this respect, animated films are not so different from most films. But animated films are often considered to be "sanitized" and devoid of sexual content or racial messaging. Our contention has been that, even when seemingly unnecessary, heterosexuality nonetheless appears within animated films and, indeed, is such a regular component of these films that we might question what would happen without its incorporation. That is, heterosexuality, even when it would seem unnecessary, is embedded within the very construction of these stories to such an extent that we might wonder whether the stories would actually crumble without it.

Far from being sanitized, we have argued, we can find heterosexual banter, desire, family formations, couples, and strivings in general within the films we have considered. In the case of *The Princess and the Frog*, we might suggest that while Princess Tiana is being anticipated as a black princess, there is nothing to indicate that she is anything but a straight princess. In fact, "the twist" itself is premised on heterosexuality insofar as Princess Tiana turns into a frog upon kissing a prince frog; that is, we still have a relationship, here, between a princess and a prince. Alternately, while many examples of friendship between men and male characters can be found within animated films, those friendships must always be clarified as *friendships only*. Same-sex relationships are clarified as heterosexual through snide comments and the emergence of (beautiful) women/female characters who garner the affections of one (or both) of the male characters in the pairing. Likewise, while examples of alternative family structures can be found within animated films, these families are only constructed as temporary and must be disbanded so that adopted members can connect with others like themselves.

SUPERFICIAL/CONTAINED ALTERNATIVES

Thus, while animated films offer moments of alternative frameworks and possibilities, such alternatives are always merely superficial ones. Particular characters or structures might appear transgressive, and specific messages within animated films might appear progressive, but such characters and messages come at a cost. Not only do such moments arise only to be reincorporated into an overall mainstream narrative, as suggested above—having their potential impact undermined—but characters that might be considered transgressive or lessons that might be considered progressive are only made possible through the use of stereotypical and otherwise problematic representations within these same films. Alternatives in one arena are made possible through exclusions and distortions in another.

Princess Tiana appears straight and interested in the prince—a black princess neatly folded and contained within the parameters of heterosexual love—but how much of her time in the film is spent in human form and how much as a frog? To what extent does her appearance as a frog—the film's twist—actually serve to downplay her blackness? To what extent does the whiteness of the prince—a possible interracial romance—rather serve to anchor the well-rehearsed story of the princess and the prince, maintaining its whiteness as a trope and an institution. To what extent must we strain our eyes to see various "alternatives," and to what extent are these very differences erased, further marginalized, and rendered impotent within this film's parameters?

COMING ATTRACTIONS

The final point we would like to address in this conclusion involves the future: where do we go from here? and what would it mean for studios working on animated films to move away from trite racial, gender, and sexual animations and problematic ideological representations? To answer the first question, we must first acknowledge that our project, though certainly broad, was not exhaustive, thus scholarly analyses should continue to provide critiques of problematic representations, tropes, and ideologies. Similarly, activists must continue to make connections between problematic representations, acknowledging that racism, sexism, and heterosexism are linked and present in these films (as they are linked and present in the broader society). And both groups must continue to complicate their critiques beyond the standard claim of stereotypical representations.

The answer to the second question is more complicated, for it would involve an effort by the animation studios to change the very essence and history of animated films. According to DreamWorks' webpage, the company "is devoted to producing high-quality family entertainment through the use of computer-generated (CG) animation," with the goal of releasing "two . . . animated feature films a year that deliver great stories, breathtaking visual imagery and a sensibility that appeals to both children and adults." Similarly, on its website, Pixar states that the company's "objective is to combine proprietary technology and world-class creative talent to develop computer-animated feature films with memorable characters and heartwarming stories that appeal to audiences of all ages." Though perhaps noble, the goal of delivering great or heartwarming stories falls short of the possibilities, as stories can only be considered great or heartwarming if they resonate with the audience, and the only way these corporations have found they are able to create stories that resonate with the audience is to constantly and consistently rehearse the same tropes and the same ideologies.

What if, instead of longing for a nuclear, heteronormative family, Lilo were taken care of by her sister and their community, which came together after the tragic death of her parents to help raise this child? What if Nemo's father did what clown fish are meant to do and switched sex, giving Nemo more siblings with whom to play? What if Lenny were accepted and loved by his family and friends from the start, even if he wanted to be a dolphin and not a shark? What if the reef didn't have a ghetto? Or an Italian mob? Or a repulsive Latina fish? Or a love story? What if *Cars* had multidimensional cars "of color?" What if *Toy Story* were a story about toys? What if Manny never found Ellie? What if he were perfectly content with his new friends/family (Sid and Diego)? Would he still be a mammoth? What if a worker ant could learn to feel important without having to fall in love with the colony's princess? And what if a princess could be a princess without a prince? What if she could become a queen and rule like no other monarch has ever ruled: with love and the interest of her people at heart? Would those stories be great? Would they be heartwarming? Would they resonate with the audience?

We believe it would be possible to craft meaningful and moving stories without employing images and narratives invested in the maintenance of heterosexual and racial norms. We even think they would speak to audiences in powerful ways. As *The Princess and the Frog* reminds us, and our analyses of animated films produced over the past two decades have underscored, however, (racial, sexual, and/or gender) difference too often makes a difference in ways that divide, diminish, exclude, rank, distort, and otherwise dehumanize, while valorizing the values, relationships, and identities central to whiteness and heterosexuality. Indeed, we have grave doubts about the emergence of a new animated cinema so long as white racial (hetero)sexist frames shape it.

BIBLIOGRAPHY

Achebe, Chinua. 1977. An image of Africa. *Massachusetts Review* 18 (4): 782–94.

Addison, E. 1993. Saving other women from other men: Disney's *Aladdin*. *Camera Obscura* 31:5–25.

Aidman, Amy. 1999. Disney's *Pocahontas*: Conversations with Native American and Euro-American girls. In *Growing up girls: Popular culture and the construction of identity*, ed. Sharon R. Mazzarella and Norma Odom Pecora, 133–58. New York: Peter Lang.

American Family Association. 2005. AFA ends Disney boycott. Retrieved Oct. 3, 2008, from http://afa.net/disney.

Amici, Randy. 2007. Pocahontas unanimated: The life of a Powhatan princess. In *Box office archaeology: Refining Hollywood's portrayal of the past*, ed. Julie M. Schablitsky, 104–29. Walnut Creek, CA: Left Coast Press.

Ansell, A. E. 1997. *New right, new racism: Race and reaction in the United States and Britain*. New York: New York University Press.

Artz, Lee. 2002. Animated hierarchy: Disney and the globalization of capitalism. *Global Media Journal* 1 (1): 1–43.

——. 2004. The righteous of self-center royals: The world according to Disney. *Journal of Cultural & Media Studies* 18 (1): 116–46.

Associated Press. 2005. A new world at Disney: Disney's new CEO Iger reflects on his style, goals, challenges. *Spokesman-Review*, Mar. 19, A11.

Ayres, Brenda, ed. 2003. *The emperor's old groove: Decolonizing Disney's Magic Kingdom.* New York: Peter Lang Publishing.

Bannon, Lisa. 1995. How a rumor spread about subliminal sex in Disney's 'Aladdin.' *Wall Street Journal*, Oct. 24. Retrieved Apr. 13, 2009, from http://www.snopes.com/disney/info/aladwsj.htm.

Barnes, Brooks. 2009. Her prince has come. Critics, too. *New York Times*, May 29. http://www.nytimes.com/2009/05/31/fashion/31disney.html?pagewanted=all.

Bell, Elizabeth, Lynda Haas, and Laura Sells, eds. 1995. *From mouse to mermaid: The politics of film, gender and culture.* Bloomington: Indiana University Press.

Berg, Charles R. 2002. *Latino images in film: Stereotypes, subversion, resistance.* Austin: University of Texas Press.

Berkhofer, Robert F. 1979. *The white man's Indian.* New York: Vintage.

BET News. 2009. Disney still in the hot seat over black princess. *BET-News.com*, June 9. http://blogs.bet.com/news/newsyoushouldknow/disney-still-in-the-hot-seat-over-black-princess.

Bonilla-Silva, Eduardo. 2003. *Racism without racists: Color-blind racism and the persistence of racial inequality in the United States.* New York: Rowman & Littlefield.

Bowles, Scott. 2005. Family films outperform R-rated at box office. *Spokesman-Review*, Mar. 17, D7.

Bryman, Alan. 2004. *The Disneyization of society.* London: Sage.

Buescher, D. T., and Kent Ono. 1996. Civilized colonialism: Pocahontas as neocolonial rhetoric. *Women's Studies in Communication* 19:127–53.

Buhler, Stephen M. 2003. Shakespeare and company: The *Lion King* and the Disneyfication of *Hamlet.* In *The Emperor's old groove: Decolonizing the Magic Kingdom,* ed. Brenda Ayres, pp. 117–30. New York: Peter Lang.

Byrne, Eleanor, and Martin McQuillan, eds. 2000. *Deconstructing Disney*. London: Pluto Press.

Caputi, Jane. 2007. Green consciousness: Earth-based myth and meaning in *Shrek*. *Ethics and the Environment* 12 (2): 23–44.

Chanter, Tina. Forthcoming. Irigaray's challenge to the fetishistic hegemony of the Platonic one and many. In *Re-writing difference: Luce Irigaray and "the Greeks,"* ed. Elena Varikas and Athena Athanasion. Albany: SUNY Press.

Coalition against Racial, Religious and Ethnic Stereotyping. 2004. National *Shark Tale* boycott. Pamphlet. Available online at http://www.osia.org/public/commission/shark_tale.asp.

Cohen, Karl F. 2004. *Forbidden animation: Censored cartoons and blacklisted animators in America*. Jefferson, NC: McFarland.

Collins, Patricia Hill. 2005. *Black sexual politics: African Americans, gender, and the new racism*. New York: Routledge.

Crary, David. 2005. Cartoon 'gays' spark real debate. *Lewiston Tribune*, Feb. 3, 2A.

Daly, Steve. 2005. Coming 'toon: A CG animation reaches a record high, the heat is on for more hits. *Entertainment Weekly*, Mar. 4, 20–22.

Denzin, Norman. 2002. *Reading race*. London: Sage.

Disney boycott. 1996. Website. Retrieved Oct. 20, 2008, from http://www.geocities.com/heartland/7547/disney.html.

Disney.com. 2009. The princess and the frog.

Do Rozario, Rebecca-Ann C. 2004. The princess and the Magic Kingdom: Beyond nostalgia, the function of the Disney princess. *Women's Studies in Communication* 27 (1): 34–59.

Downey, S. D. 1996. Feminine empowerment in Disney's *Beauty and the Beast*. *Women's Studies in Communication* 19 (2): 185–212.

DreamWorks. 2009. Company overview. http://www.dreamworksanimation.com.

Dundes, Lauren. 2001. Disney's modern heroine Pocahontas: Revealing age-old gender stereotypes and role discontinuity under a façade of liberation. *Social Science Journal* 38 (3): 353–65.

Edgerton, Gary, and Kathy Merlock Jackson. 1996. Redesigning Pocahontas: Disney, the white man's Indian, and the marketing of dreams. *Journal of Popular Film and Television* 24 (2): 90–98.

Faherty, Vincent E. 2001. Is the mouse sensitive? A study of race, gender, and social vulnerability in Disney animated films. *SIMILE* 1 (3): 1–8.

Feagin, Joe R. 2001. *Racist America: Roots, current realities, and future reparations.* New York: Routledge.

——. 2006. *Systemic racism: A theory of oppression.* New York: Routledge.

——. 2009. *The white racial frame: Centuries of racial framing and counter-framing.* New York: Routledge.

Feagin, Joe R., Hernán Vera, and Pinar Batur. 2001. *White racism.* New York: Routledge.

Forgacs, D. 1992. Disney animation and the business of childhood. *Screen* 33 (4): 361–74.

Freeman, Elizabeth. 2005. Monsters, Inc.: Notes on the neoliberal arts education. *New Literary History* 36 (1): 83–95.

Giese, Paula. 1996. Native opinions on Pocahontas. Available online at http://www.kstrom.net/isk/poca/pocahont.html.

Giroux, Henry. 1994. *Disturbing pleasures: Learning popular culture.* New York: Routledge.

——. 1999. *The mouse that roared: Disney and the end of innocence.* Lanham, MD: Rowman & Littlefield.

Goldberg, David Theo. 2002. *The racial state.* Oxford: Blackwell.

Gooding-Williams, Robert. 2006. *Look a negro! Philosophical essays on race, culture and politics.* New York: Routledge.

Griffin, Sean. 1994. The illusion of 'identity': Gender and racial representation in *Aladdin. Animation Journal* 3 (1): 64–73.

——. 2000. *Tinker Belles and evil queens: The Walt Disney Company from the inside out.* New York: New York University Press.

Halberstam, Judith. 2008. Animating revolution/revolting animation: Penguin love, doll sex and the spectacle of the queer nonhuman. In *Queering the Non/Human,* ed. Noreen Giffney and Myra J. Hird, 265–81. Burlington, VT: Ashgate.

Hale, G. E. 1999. *Making whiteness: The culture of segregation in the South, 1890–1940.* New York: Random House.

Hall, S. 1991. Brave new world: The debate about post-Fordism. *Socialist Review* 21 (1): 57–64.

Hardt, Michael, and Antonio Negri. 2001. *Empire.* Cambridge, MA: Harvard University Press.

Hendry, Joy. 2000. *The Orient strikes back: A global view of cultural display*. Oxford: Berg.

Henke, Jill Birnie, and Diane Zimmerman Umble. 1999. And she lived happily ever after. . . . The Disney myth in the video age. In *Mediated women: Representations in popular culture*, ed. Marian Myers, 321–37. Cresskill, NJ: Hampton Press.

Hoerner, K. L. 1996. Gender roles in Disney films: Analyzing behaviors from Snow White to Simba. *Women's Studies in Communication* 19:213–28.

Jacobsen, E., and A. Dulsrud. 2007. Will consumers save the world? The framing of political consumerism. *Journal of Agricultural and Environmental Ethics* 20 (5): 469–82.

Johnston, J. 2008. The citizen-consumer hybrid: Ideological tensions and the case of Whole Foods Market. *Theory and Society* 37 (3): 229–70.

Kasturi, Sumana. 2002. Constructing childhood in a corporate world: Cultural studies, childhood, and Disney. In *Kidworld: Childhood studies, global perspectives, and education*, ed. Gaile S. Cannella and Joe L. Kincheloe, 39–58. New York: Peter Lang.

Kellner, Douglas. 1995. *Media culture*. New York: Routledge.

Kilpatrick, Jacquelyn. 1999. *Celluloid Indians: Native Americans and film*. Lincoln: University of Nebraska Press.

Kim, M., and A. Y. Chung. 2005. Consuming Orientalism: Images of Asian/American women in multicultural advertising. *Qualitative Sociology* 28 (1): 67–91.

King, C. R., and C. F. Springwood, eds. 2001. *Team spirits: The Native American mascot controversy*. Lincoln: University of Nebraska Press.

Krech, Shepard. 1999. *The ecological Indian: Myth and history*. New York: Norton.

Kuenz, J. 1993. It's a small world after all: Disney and the pleasures of identification. *South Atlantic Quarterly* 92 (1): 63–88.

Lacroix, Celeste. 2004. Images of animated others: The Orientalization of Disney's cartoon heroines from *The Little Mermaid* to *The Hunchback of Notre Dame*. *Popular Communication* 2 (4): 213–29.

Lawrence, Elizabeth Atwood. 1985. *Hoofbeats and society: Studies of human-horse interactions*. Bloomington: Indiana University Press.

Lawson, Andrea, and Gregory Fouts. 2004. Mental illness in Disney animated films. *Canadian Journal of Psychiatry* 49 (5): 310–13.

Li-Vollmer, Meredith, and Mark E. LaPointe. 2004. Gender transgression and villainy in animated films. *Journal of Popular Communication* 1 (2): 89.

Lugo-Lugo, Carmen R. 2004. Better than Crest: The selective whitening and mainstreaming of Latinos in the United States (the case of popular culture). In *Racial crossroads: A reader in comparative ethnic studies*, ed. Yolanda F. Niemann et al., 393–404. Dubuque, IA: Kendall/Hunt Publishing Company.

Lurry, Celia. 1996. *Consumer culture*. Oxford: Blackwell.

Ma, Sheing-mei. 2000. Yellow Kung Fu and black jokes. *Television and New Media* 1 (2): 239–44.

Macleod, Dianne Sachko. 2003. The politics of vision: Disney, *Aladdin*, and the Gulf War. In *The emperor's old groove: Decolonizing Disney's Magic Kingdom*, ed. Brenda Ayers, 179–92. New York: Peter Lang.

Manring, M. M. 1998. *Slave in a box: The strange career of Aunt Jemima*. Charlottesville: University of Virginia Press.

Martin, Karin A., and Emily Kazyak. 2009. Hetero-romantic love and heterosexiness in children's G-rated films. *Gender and Society* 23 (3): 315–36.

Martín-Rodríguez, Manuel M. 1999. Reel origins: Multiculturalism, history, and the American children's movie. In *The American child: A cultural studies reader*, ed. Caroline F. Levander and Carol J. Singley, 280–302. New Brunswick, NJ: Rutgers University Press.

——. 2000. Hyenas in the pride lands: Latinos/as and immigration in Disney's *The Lion King*. *Aztlan* 25 (1): 47–66.

——. 2003. *Life in search of readers: Reading (in) Chicano/a literature*. Albuquerque: University of New Mexico Press.

Mayer, Ruth. 2002. *Artificial Africas: Colonial images in the times of globalization*. Hanover, NH: Dartmouth College Press.

Mazrui, Ali A. 2005. The re-invention of Africa: Edward Said, V. Y. Mudimbe, and beyond. *Research in African Literature* 36 (3): 68–82.

McClintock, A. 1995. *Imperial leather: Race, gender, and sexuality in the colonial contest*. New York: Routledge.

Micheletti, M. 2003. *Political virtue and shopping: Individuals, consumerism, and collective action*. New York: Palgrave Macmillan.

Micheletti, M., A. Føllesdal, and D. Stolle, eds. 2004. *Politics, products, and markets: Exploring political consumerism past and present*. New Brunswick, NJ: Transaction Publishers.

Michira, James. 2002. Images of Africa in the western media. Retrieved Mar. 12, 2009, from http://www.teachingliterature.org/teaching literature/pdf/multi/images_of_africa_michira.pdf.

Mills, Charles. 1997. *The racial contract*. Ithaca, NY: Cornell University Press.

Miranda, Carolina A., and Logan Orlando. 2005. Don't ask, don't tell. *Time*, Jan. 31, 20.

Mitchell, Lee Clark. 2003. Whose West is it anyway? or, What's myth got to do with it? The role of "America" in the creation of the myth of the West. *American Review of Canadian Studies* 33:497–508.

Monbiot, George. 2004. Of mice and money men: The sinister grip that Disney exerts on children's imaginations may finally loosen. *Guardian*, Feb. 17, 19.

Mudimbe, V. Y. 1988. *The invention of Africa: Gnosis, philosophy, and the order of knowledge*. Durham, NC: Duke University Press.

Noriega, C. A. 2000. *Shot in America: Television, the state and the rise of Chicano cinema*. Minneapolis: University of Minnesota Press.

O'Brien, P. C. 1996. The happiest films on Earth: A textual and contextual analysis of Walt Disney's *Cinderella* and *The Little Mermaid*. *Women's Studies in Communication* 19:155–91.

Ono, Kent, and D. T. Buescher. 2001. Deciphering Pocahontas: Unpackaging the commodification of a Native American Woman. *Critical Studies in Communication* 18:23–43.

Ostman, Ronald E. 1996. Disney and its conservative critics: Images versus realities. *Journal of Popular Film and Television* 24 (2): 82–89.

Parekh, Pushpa Naidu. 2003. *Pocahontas*: The Disney imaginary. In *The emperor's old groove: Decolonizing Disney's Magic Kingdom*, ed. Brenda Ayers, 167–78. New York: Peter Lang.

Pewewardy, Cornell D. 1996. The Pocahontas paradox: A cautionary tale for educators. *Journal of Navajo Education* 14:20–25.

Piana, Libero Della. 2004. *Shark Tale* controversy: Are Italian Americans the new anti-racist front? Retrieved Sept. 10, 2008, from http://www.blackcommentator.com/109/109_italians.html.

Pixar. 2009. Corporate overview. http://www.pixar.com/companyinfo/about_us/overview.htm.

Rosaldo, Renato. 1989. *Culture and truth: The remaking of social analysis.* Boston: Beacon Press.

Sardar, Ziauddin. 2002. Walt Disney and the double victimization of Pocahontas. In *The third text reader on art, culture, and theory,* ed. Rasheed Araeen, Sean Cubitt, and Ziauddin Sardar, 193–203. New York: Continuum.

Shortsleeve, Kevin. 2004. The wonderful world of the Depression: Disney, despotism, and the 1930s or why Disney scares us. *Lion and the Unicorn* 26 (1): 1–30.

Shreve, Jenn. 1997. Dissing Disney. *Metroactive* Sept. 25. Retrieved May 30, 2009, from http://www.metroactive.com/papers/metro/09.25.97/disney-9739.html.

Silverman, Helaine. 2002. Groovin' to ancient Peru: A critical analysis of Disney's *The Emperor's New Groove. Journal of Social Archaeology* 2 (3): 298–322.

Smith, Leef. 1995. Disney's loin king? Group sees dirt in the dust. *Washington Post,* Sept. 1. Retrieved Oct. 20, 2008, from http://www.washingtonpost.com/wp-srv/style/longterm/review96/flionking.htm.

Smoodin, Eric, ed. 1994. *Disney discourse: Producing the Magic Kingdom.* New York: Routledge.

Sreedhar, Suhas. 2009. Animation nation, part I: Dreamworks goes to Bangalore. *IEEE Spectrum* (May). Retrieved June 1, 2009, from http://www.spectrum.ieee.org/computing/software/animation-nation-part-i-dreamworks-goes-to-bangalore.

Strong, Pauline Turner. 1996. Animated Indians: Critique and contradiction in commodified children's culture. *Cultural Anthropology* 11 (3): 405–24.

Tanner, Litsa Renee, Shelley A. Haddock, Toni Schindler Zimmerman, and Lori K. Lund. 2003. Images of couples and families in Disney feature-length films. *American Journal of Family Therapy* 31:355–73.

Tezcatlipoca, Olin. 2000. Road to El Dorado has no respect for history. Retrieved Oct. 10, 2008, from http://bluecorncomics.com/eldorado.htm.

The 25 most controversial movies ever. *Entertainment Weekly.* Retrieved Mar. 16, 2008, from http://www.ew.com/ew/article/0,,1202224,00 .html.

Tompkins, Jane. 1992. *West of everything: The inner life of Westerns.* New York: Oxford University Press.

Towbin, Mia Adessa, Shelley A. Haddock, Toni Schindler Zimmerman, Lori K. Lund, and Litsa Renee Tanner. 2003. Images of gender, race, age and sexual orientation in Disney feature-length animated films. *Journal of Feminist Family Therapy* 15 (4): 19–44.

Tseelon, E. 1995. *The Little Mermaid:* An icon of woman's condition in patriarchy and the human condition of castration. *International Journal of Psychoanalysis* 76 (5): 1017–30.

U.S. Census Bureau. 2000. http://www.census.gov/statab/ranks/rank10.txt.

van Gelder, Lawrence. 2004. Arts briefing: War of words. *New York Times.* Retrieved May 13, 2009, from http://www.nytimes.com/2004/ 09/14/arts/14arts.htm.

Vasquez, Sara. 2000. An open letter on *The Road to El Dorado.* Retrieved Oct. 10, 2008, from http://bluecorncomics.com/eldorado.htm.

Vera, Hernan, and Andrew M. Gordon. 2003. *Screen saviors: Hollywood fictions of whiteness.* Lanham, MD: Rowman & Littlefield.

Wainer, A. 1993. Reversal of roles: Subversion and reaffirmation of racial stereotypes in *Dumbo* and *The Jungle Book. Synch* 1:50–57.

Ward, Annalee R. 1993. *The Lion King's* mythic narrative. *Journal of Popular Film and Television* 23:171–78.

———. 2002. *Mouse morality: The rhetoric of Disney animated film.* Austin: University of Texas Press.

Wasko, Janet. 2001. *Understanding Disney.* Cambridge: Polity Press.

Wasko, Janet, Mark Phillips, and Eileen R. Meehan. 2001. *Dazzled by Disney? The global Disney audiences project.* Leicester, UK: Leicester University Press.

Watts, Steven. 1997. *The Magic Kingdom: Walt Disney and the American way of life.* Boston: Houghton Mifflin Company.

White, Susan. 1993. Split skins: Female agency and bodily mutilation in *The Little Mermaid.* In *Film theory goes to the movies,* ed. Jim Collins, Hillary Radner, and Ava Preacher Collins, 182–95. New York: Routledge.

White, T. R., and J. E. Winn. 1998. Islam, animation, and money: The reception of Disney's *Aladdin* in Southeast Asia. In *Themes and issues in Asian cartooning*, ed. J. A. Lent, 61–76. Bowling Green, OH: Bowling Green University Press.

Whitley, David. 2008. *The idea of nature in Disney animation*. Aldershot, Hampshire: Ashgate Publishing.

Willis, Susan. 1995. I want the black one: Is there a place for Afro-American culture in commodity culture? In *Cultural remix: Theories of politics and the popular*, ed. E. Carter, J. Donald, and J. Squires, 141–66. London: Lawrence & Wishart.

Wingfield, Marvin, and Bushara Karaman. 1995. Arab stereotypes and American educators. Retrieved June 17, 2008, from http://www.adc.org/index.php?283.

Wise, Christopher. 2003. Notes from the *Aladdin* industry: or, Middle Eastern folklore in the era of multinational capitalism. In *The emperor's old groove: Decolonizing Disney's Magic Kingdom*, ed. Brenda Ayers, 105–14. New York: Peter Lang.

Yellow Bird, Michael. 2004. Cowboys and Indians: Toys of genocide, icons of American colonialism. *Wicazo SA Review* Fall, 33–48.

Zhang, Keen. 2008. 'Artist' calls for Pandaland boycott of Kung Fu Panda. Retrieved Sept. 12, 2008, from http://www.china.org.cn/culture/2008-06/20/content_15863889.htm.

FILMOGRAPHY

Aladdin. Dirs. Ron Clements and John Musker. Walt Disney Feature Animation and Walt Disney Pictures, 1992.

Antz. Dirs. Eric Darnell and Tim Johnson. DreamWorks SKG and Pacific Data Images, 1998.

Atlantis: The Lost Empire. Dirs. Gary Trousdale and Kirk Wise. Toon City, Walt Disney Feature Animation, and Walt Disney Pictures, 2001.

Beauty and the Beast. Dirs. Gary Trousdale and Kirk Wise. Silver Screen Partners IV and Walt Disney Pictures, 1991.

Brother Bear. Dirs. Aaron Blaise and Robert Walker. Walt Disney Feature Animation and Walt Disney Pictures, 2003.

Bug's Life, A. Dirs. John Lasseter and Andrew Stanton. Pixar Animation Studios and Walt Disney Pictures, 1998.

Cars. Dirs. John Lasseter and Joe Ranft. Walt Disney Pictures and Pixar Animation Studios, 2006.

Chicken Run. Dirs. Peter Lord and Nick Park. DreamWorks SKG, Pathé Pictures International, and Aardman Animations, 2000.

Cinderella. Dirs. Clyde Geronimi, Wilfred Jackson, and Hamilton Luske. Walt Disney Productions, 1950.

Dinosaur. Dirs. Eric Leighton and Ralph Zondag. Walt Disney Feature Animation and Walt Disney Pictures, 2000.

Dumbo. Dir. Ben Sharpsteen. Walt Disney Productions, 1941.

Emperor's New Groove, The. Dir. Mark Dindal. Walt Disney Animation and Walt Disney Pictures, 2000.

Fantasia. Dir. James Algar et al. Walt Disney Pictures and Walt Disney Productions, 1940.

Finding Nemo. Dirs. Andrew Stanton and Lee Unkrich. Walt Disney Pictures, Pixar Animation Studios, and Disney Enterprises, 2003.

Happy Feet. Dirs. George Miller, Warren Coleman, and Judy Morris. Kingdom Feature Productions, Animal Logic, Kennedy Miller Productions, and Village Roadshow Pictures, 2006.

Hercules. Dirs. Ron Clements and John Musker. Walt Disney Pictures and Walt Disney Feature Animation, 1997.

Home on the Range. Dirs. Will Finn and John Sanford. Walt Disney Pictures and Walt Disney Feature Animation, 2004.

Hunchback of Notre Dame, The. Dirs. Gary Trousdale and Kirk Wise. Walt Disney Feature Animation and Walt Disney Pictures, 1996.

Ice Age. Dirs. Chris Wedge and Carlos Saldanha. Blue Sky Studios and Twentieth Century Fox Animation, 2002.

Ice Age: Dawn of the Dinosaurs. Dirs. Carlos Saldanha and Mike Thurmeier. Blue Sky Studios and Twentieth Century Fox Animation, 2009.

Incredibles, The. Dir. Brad Bird. Walt Disney Pictures and Pixar Animation Studios, 2004.

Joseph: King of Dreams. Dirs. Rob LaDuca and Robert C. Ramierez. DreamWorks Home Entertainment and Universal Home Video, 2000.

Jungle Book, The. Dir. Wolfgang Reitherman. Walt Disney Productions, 1967.

Kung Fu Panda. Dirs. Mark Osborne and John Stevenson. DreamWorks Animation and Pacific Data Images, 2008.

Lady and the Tramp. Dirs. Clyde Geronimi, Wilfred Jackson, and Hamilton Luske. Walt Disney Pictures, 1955.

Lilo and Stitch. Dirs. Dean DeBlois and Chris Sanders. Walt Disney Feature Animation and Walt Disney Pictures, 2002.

Lion King, The. Dirs. Roger Allers and Rob Minkoff. Walt Disney Feature Animation and Walt Disney Pictures, 1994.

Little Mermaid, The. Dirs. Ron Clements and John Musker. Walt Disney Pictures and Silver Screen Partners IV, 1989.

Madagascar. Dirs. Eric Darnell and Tom McGrath. DreamWorks SKG, Pacific Data Images, and DreamWorks Animation, 2005.

Madagascar: Escape 2 Africa. Dirs. Eric Darnell and Tom McGrath. DreamWorks Animation and Pacific Data Images, 2008.

Monsters Inc. Dirs. Pete Docter, David Silverman, and Lee Unkrich. Pixar Animation Studios and Walt Disney Pictures, 2001.

Mulan. Dirs. Tony Bancroft and Barry Cook. Walt Disney Feature Animation and Walt Disney Pictures, 1998.

Pocahontas. Dirs. Mike Gabriel and Eric Goldberg. Walt Disney Feature Animation and Walt Disney Pictures, 1995.

Prince of Egypt, The. Dirs. Brenda Chapman, Steve Hickner, and Simon Wells. DreamWorks SKG, 1998.

Princess and the Frog, The. Dirs. Ron Clements and John Musker. Walt Disney Animation Studios and Walt Disney Pictures, 2009.

Road to El Dorado, The. Dirs. Bibo Bergeron, Will Finn, Don Paul, and David Silverman. DreamWorks SKG and Stardust Pictures, 2000.

Shark Tale. Dirs. Bibo Bergeron, Vicky Jenson, and Rob Letterman. DreamWorks Animation, DreamWorks SKG, and Pacific Data Images, 2004.

Shrek. Dirs. Andrew Adamson and Vicky Jenson. DreamWorks Animation, DreamWorks SKG, and Pacific Data Images, 2001.

Shrek 2. Dirs. Andrew Adamson, Kelly Asbury, and Conrad Vernon. DreamWorks SKG, Pacific Data Images, and DreamWorks Animation, 2004.

Sinbad: Legend of the Seven Seas. Dirs. Patrick Gilmore and Tim Johnson. DreamWorks Animation, DreamWorks Pictures, DreamWorks SKG, and Stardust Pictures, 2003.

Sleeping Beauty. Dir. Clyde Geronimi. Walt Disney Productions, 1959.

Snow White. Dir. David Hand. Walt Disney Productions, 1937.

Song of the South. Dirs. Harve Foster and Wilfred Jackson. Walt Disney Productions, 1946.

Spirit: Stallion of the Cimarron. Dirs. Kelly Asbury and Lorna Cook. Dreamworks Animation and DreamWorks SKG, 2002.

Tarzan. Dirs. Chris Buck and Kevin Lima. Walt Disney Pictures, Edgar Rice Burroughs, Inc., and Walt Disney Feature Animation, 1999.

Toy Story. Dir. John Lasseter. Walt Disney Pictures and Pixar Animation Studios, 1995.

Toy Story 2. Dirs. John Lasseter, Ash Brannon, and Lee Unkrich. Pixar Animation Studios and Walt Disney Pictures, 1999.

Up. Dirs. Pete Docter and Bob Peterson. Walt Disney Pictures and Pixar Animation Studios, 2009.

INDEX

ABOUT THE AUTHORS

Mary K. Bloodsworth-Lugo is associate professor of comparative ethnic studies at Washington State University. She has taught and published in the areas of race and ethnicity, gender and sexuality, theories of the body, identity, popular culture, and contemporary continental political philosophy. Bloodsworth-Lugo is author of *In-Between Bodies: Sexual Difference, Race, and Sexuality* and co-editor, with Carmen R. Lugo-Lugo, of *A New Kind of Containment: "The War on Terror," Race, and Sexuality*. Her recent work on U.S. administrative rhetoric and "the War on Terror," with Carmen R. Lugo-Lugo, has also appeared in *Peace & Change, International Journal of Contemporary Sociology, Reconstruction, Peace Review, Cultural Studies*, and *Journal of African American Studies*. Their co-authored book, *Containing (Un)American Bodies: Race, Sexuality, and Post-September 11th Constructions of Citizenship*, is currently in progress.

C. Richard King is professor and chair of comparative ethnic studies at Washington State University. He has written extensively on the changing contours of race in post-civil-rights America. His work has appeared a variety of journals, including *American Indian Culture and Research Journal, Journal of Sport and Social Issues, Public Historian, Qualitative Inquiry,* and *Colorlines Magazine.* He is also the author/editor of several books, including *Team Spirits: The Native American Mascot Controversy* (a CHOICE 2001 Outstanding Academic Title), *Postcolonial America,* and more recently *Native American Athletes in Sport and Society.* Presently, he is at work on a monograph (with David J. Leonard) analyzing the production and consumption of media culture within white nationalist communities.

Carmen R. Lugo-Lugo is associate professor of comparative ethnic studies at Washington State University, and is engaged in research on empire, "the War on Terror," and popular culture. She has co-authored, with Mary K. Bloodsworth-Lugo, several articles on the rhetoric behind "the War on Terror" and its link to discourse surrounding various groups. She has published several articles on the representation of Latinos and other minoritized groups within U.S. popular culture. Lugo-Lugo is currently revising a manuscript titled *An Island of Coloniality: Women, Vieques, and the Invisibility of the Third World Commonwealth of Puerto Rico* and co-writing, with Mary K. Bloodsworth-Lugo, a book titled *Containing (Un)American Bodies: Race, Sexuality, and Post-September 11th Constructions of Citizenship.* Their edited volume *A New Kind of Containment: "The War on Terror," Race, and Sexuality* was published by Rodopi Press in 2009.